CANADIAN HISTORICAL CONTROVERSIES

Series Editor
W. J. ECCLES

Department of History, University of Toronto

BRITISH ATTITUDES TOWARDS CANADA, 1822-1849

PETER BURROUGHS

Department of History
Dalhousie University, Halifax, Nova Scotia

PRENTICE-HALL   **p**   OF CANADA, LTD.

Scarborough,   **h**   Ontario

© 1971 by Prentice-Hall of Canada, Ltd.
Scarborough, Ontario

PRENTICE-HALL, INC., ENGLEWOOD CLIFFS, NEW JERSEY
PRENTICE-HALL INTERNATIONAL, INC., LONDON
PRENTICE-HALL OF AUSTRALIA, PTY., LTD., SYDNEY
PRENTICE-HALL OF INDIA, PVT., LTD., NEW DELHI
PRENTICE-HALL OF JAPAN, INC., TOKYO

Library of Congress Catalog Card No. 70-134455
0-13-083139-5 Pa
0-13-083147-6 Cl
1 2 3 4 5 75 74 73 72 71
PRINTED IN CANADA

Contents

Series Editor's Preface

The aim of this series is to compare and to subject to critical scrutiny, the ways in which historians have treated major issues in Canadian history. Each volume defines one issue in space and time, and indicates its importance for both the people concerned and later generations. Selected quotations from contemporary sources indicate the views of the people of the period; then, the historians' interpretations of the issue are given and discussed critically. Finally, the author indicates what needs to be done, pointing out, wherever possible, evidence not yet utilized or inadequately examined by earlier historians, and suggests new lines of approach that could place the issue in a more revealing light.

It is hoped that in this way the student of history will gain, not only a better understanding of the events, but also an insight into the way in which history is written. He will, it is hoped, become aware that there is no such thing as "definitive history," that the history of this country was not brought down the mountain engraved on ten stone tablets by certain eminent scholars whose opinions cannot be questioned. Events in a historian's own time influence the way in which he views the past, the questions he asks of it, the methods he employs in seeking the answers, and the values that govern his judgements. Thus, what the historian has written has continually to be subjected to critical examination and his interpretations qualified or revised.

If this series enables those interested in the history of Canada to approach it more critically, with a better appreciation of what has been done, and a clearer idea of what needs to be done, it will have served its purpose.

W. J. E.

Introduction

Because of an understandable preoccupation with indigenous North American forces and tendencies, Canadian historians writing about the century between the conquest and confederation have often paid insufficient attention to the character of British colonial policy and the nature of English opinion concerning overseas possessions. Yet every facet of Canadian economic and political development during these years, and many aspects of the country's social and religious history, were profoundly influenced by British attitudes and policies. The ideas and actions of politicians in distant Westminster and administrators in the recesses of Downing Street were significant for Canadians. This book is therefore written in the confident belief that Canadian history in the colonial period is not fully intelligible without some understanding of the wider imperial context, the changing nature of British policies, and the underlying opinions of Englishmen concerning the empire in North America.

The years from 1822 to 1849 covered by this book not only represent a crucial period in the development of Canada and the British empire, but also possess a certain unity. During these years, the colonial system on which the old American empire had been founded gradually disintegrated; more liberal political and economic principles were advocated and finally accepted as the basis of a new kind of relationship between Britain and Canada. In the political and constitutional field, the defects of imperal administration both in Britain and in the North American colonies were fully discerned, widely criticized, and largely remedied. With the acceptance of 'responsible government', a means was found of reconciling the colonists' desire for a greater control over their own internal affairs with the continued unity of the empire. This problem had been posed but not successfully resolved at the time of the American Revolution. Economically, the monopolies and restrictions that had characterized Britain's traditional commercial system gave way, first to the principles of reciprocity and imperial preference under the reforms of Frederick Robinson and William Huskisson in the 1820's, and then to the adoption of free trade twenty years later. Meanwhile, thousands of emigrants travelled from the British

Isles to North America; numerous theories and schemes were propagated for the more effective colonization of the spacious lands of the colonies; and British merchants and capitalists eagerly sought profitable opportunities for trade and investment within the bounds of the expanding empire.

The far-reaching changes during this period were prefaced and accompanied by vigorous public debate amongst Englishmen concerning the nature, value, and future of the British empire. This discussion embraced many facets of imperial activity and encompassed territorial possessions and commercial interests that were scattered throughout the globe. Because of the concern amongst contemporaries for general, as well as regional or particular, imperial problems, the following selection of documentary material and the accompanying analysis of historical writings do not relate exclusively to British North America, but deliberately reflect the wider background of the empire at large; a background against which English attitudes and policies towards Canada can be most instructively set. North America remained, however, at the forefront of contemporary debate over colonial affairs during the period under consideration because of its size and potential, its large and increasing British population, and its fearful proximity to the United States.

As a survey of contemporary British discussion, this book is not designed to provide a general account of Canadian history and domestic politics during those years. This information is familiar and easily accessible. Some attention is given to broad trends in British policy and imperial relations, with special reference to the growth of free trade and local self-government. We are primarily concerned, however, with English opinion regarding colonies in general and British North America in particular. For if the course of Canadian political and economic development was materially influenced by British policies, those policies were in turn shaped by prevailing English attitudes to colonial possessions. Admittedly, varying British economic requirements, changing conditions in different parts of the empire, and other elements contributed towards the formation and character of imperial designs; but those designs also reflected the views and preconceptions of the politicians and administrators concerned. Policy took shape and decisions were made in a climate of opinion, created by differing points of view and intermittent public debate, which was influential even when opinion was not especially well informed. The views of Englishmen on the topic of colonies, therefore, form a basic ingredient

vi

of Canadian history in the nineteenth century and an essential part of the historical context within which Anglo-Canadian relations must be studied.

With these considerations in mind, this book will examine three general questions: What did Englishmen consider to be the value of Britain's North American possessions? What did they think about the nature of Britain's political and economic relationship with these colonies? What were their views on the future of the British empire in North America? In Part 1 of the book these questions are explored by citing what some writers and public figures of the day thought about the issues involved. Parts 2 and 3 analyse what historians have subsequently written about the character and influence of contemporary opinion. It is hoped that the similarities and divergencies between the views of contemporaries and those of later historians will incidentally indicate something about the nature of history, the use of historical evidence, and the reasons for changes in the prevailing pattern of historical interpretation.

Grateful acknowledgment is made for permission to quote extracts from the Elgin-Grey Papers and other manuscript collections in the possession of the Public Archives of Canada. Transcripts of Crown-copyright records in the Public Record Office appear by permission of the Controller of H. M. Stationery Office. In the survey of historical writings, extensive direct quotation from books and articles has deliberately been avoided in favour of paraphrase and summarization. Since much of this summary is necessarily derivative, it is hoped that the historians concerned will accept as sufficient acknowledgment this general expression of the author's gratitude for the instruction and pleasure their writings have afforded.

P.B.

PART 1

The Contemporary Debate

A survey of British opinion on colonies in the second quarter of the nineteenth century is necessarily restricted to the views of those individuals engaged in some aspect of political life or literary pursuits who were sufficiently articulate to express their opinions and who had the desire and opportunity to record them. This is less of a limitation than might at first appear, because these were precisely the people who took decisions in the field of politics and administration or who debated those decisions, and did so largely without reference to the wishes and interests of the masses. Moreover, it was the people involved in public life who created the general climate of English opinion, and insofar as members of the working classes entertained opinions on public issues, these were derived from, or at least profoundly influenced by, the views of the leaders of society. With some justification, therefore, the following selections concentrate on the views of leading politicians, administrators, economists, and writers, and these can legitimately be claimed as representative of contemporary British opinion.

But to what extent was the 'thinking public' interested in colonies and colonial affairs in the years between 1822 and 1849? While the writings and speeches of the day may give some indication of the degree of information or ignorance on these topics, they do not offer a reliable guide to the state of public interest, since the quantity of references to colonial matters cannot be equated with the amount of apathy or concern. Many contemporaries who were professionally engaged or exceptionally interested in colonial affairs claimed that Englishmen of their day were indifferent to colonies; certainly the issues of domestic politics received greater attention from the British public. Some historians have accordingly described the second and third quarters of the nineteenth century as an age of 'anti-imperialism', when most Englishmen were indifferent or hostile to colonial possessions and regarded them as valueless and as sources of needless expense. Yet the comments of contemporaries may simply indicate that colonies were normally taken for granted by the British public, because their affairs were remote and unfamiliar. Public reaction to such crises as that presented by the Canadian rebellions in 1837 suggests that Englishmen deeply valued colonies and would not have been indifferent to the possibility of their surrender or loss, even though in less anxious times the recital of colonial grievances aroused no positive public response.

Moreover, opinion must not be studied and analysed in a vacuum, unrelated to what actually happened and divorced from policy and action. The fact is that the British empire steadily expanded, both territorially and commercially, during the period of so-called 'anti-imperialism'. This inescapable fact suggests several possibilities: that the supporters of empire were more influential than its critics or better located to influence governmental policies; that politicians and administrators were able to formulate policies without much regard to popular scepticism or hostility to colonies; or that developments overseas and on the frontiers of the empire exerted inexorable pressures that ministers and officials in London could not effectively withstand. All three explanations are valid, and clearly demonstrate how unrealistic it would be to study British opinion concerning colonies without constantly measuring and assessing it against the actual course of events.

Considerations of space naturally impose a limitation on the number and variety of documentary extracts that can be included in a book of this nature. An attempt has been made to offer a representative selection of differing English attitudes to British North America, and to indicate the diversity of opinion on the more important issues in Anglo-Canadian relations. Historians have traditionally discerned several distinct points of view and interest groups amongst British politicians, economists, and writers of the period, and to these have been attached such labels as 'anti-imperialists', 'radical imperialists', 'colonial reformers', 'philosophical radicals', 'Benthamites', and the 'Manchester school'. It would be impossible to represent the views of all these groups on each particular topic; these categories and labels are highly misleading and ought to be discarded.

The following collection of documentary material is drawn from a number of major sources. To assess the validity and importance of the views expressed, it is essential to take into consideration such matters as the occasion and circumstances of the remarks, the audience to which they were addressed, the purpose or effect they were designed to achieve, as well as the political standpoint and personal preconceptions of their author. This necessitates some awareness of the value and limitations of the different sources of historical evidence. Many of the extracts are taken, for example, from British parliamentary debates reported in the volumes of *Hansard*. Here the views of speakers are for the most part moderately expressed and not very revealing, since inmost thoughts on issues under discussion and the real motives of political activity were usually subordinated in the attempt to establish or counter a debating point, win a crucial division, or maintain or defeat a ministry. To a considerable degree, colonial questions were discussed in parliament with party political interests foremost in mind rather than on their own intrinsic merits.

A more uninhibited expression of opinion can be found in contemporary newspapers and journals, though editorial discussion of colonial questions in the daily press was infrequent at least before 1837 and usually occasioned by debates in parliament. Because of their wide readership amongst the thinking public, the leading quarterlies and journals have long been recognized as influential instruments for the expression of opinion in the nineteenth century, with the *Edinburgh Review*, predominantly Whig in its political views, the *Quarterly Review*, Tory, and the *Westminster Review*, radical. Newspapers, however, remain a relatively neglected source for opinions on the empire because historians have dismissed them as ill-informed, extravagantly written, rabidly partisan, and subject to the dominance and financial pressures of particular political groups. Yet they shaped the views and reinforced the prejudices of an important public, and probably reflected the attitudes of their readers to a far greater extent than has hitherto been acknowledged. *The Times* professed an exceptional degree of independence in its opinions, and denounced all parties in turn with a characteristic boldness and sarcasm. Amongst the London papers with a national circulation, the Tory point of view was expressed by the *Morning Herald*, the *Morning Post*, and the *Standard*, while the Whig case was presented by the *Morning Chronicle*, the *Sun*, and the *Courier*. The *Morning Advertiser* and the *Globe* tended to be more liberal in outlook, and the radicals were represented by such weeklies as the *Examiner*, the *Spectator*, and the *Colonial Gazette*.

Other sources canvassed for the present collection include the official correspondence and papers of the Colonial Office. Written in a guarded and uniquely vague style, the despatches sent from London to the governors in British North America covered all the major aspects of Anglo-Canadian relations, though the explanation of policies and decisions was usually accomplished with a minimum of reference to the individual opinions of the politicians and administrators concerned. The expression of personal views appears more frequently in minutes and memoranda written by officials, though these are seldom very frank or extensive. The private papers of the Third Earl Grey and other leading politicians of the period have also yielded a few extracts; and here where colonial issues were discussed privately with friends and colleagues, opinions were often expressed with less reserve than in the more public forms of communication. Some contemporary books and pamphlets have also been quoted, but much of this material is ephemeral or excessively detailed. Extracts from Lord Durham's *Report on the Affairs of British North America* have not been included because this crucial document should be read in its entirety in conjunction with this volume. An attempt has been made to avoid the duplication of documentary material used in the author's book, *The Colonial Reformers and Canada* (Toronto, 1969).

In conformity with the three questions posed in the Introduction, the documentary material in this section has been organized in three parts, and the individual extracts have been linked where appropriate with a connecting commentary. Section I of Part 1 discusses the value of the colonies in North America, both commercially and as fields for colonization, the respective merits of tariff protection or free trade as the basis of Britain's commercial policy, and imperial expenditure on civil, military, and ecclesiastical establishments in North America. Section II examines the problems of colonial government, with particular reference to the Canadian crisis in the thirties and the progress of local self-government in the forties. Section III deals with contemporary opinion on the future of the empire in North America, the forces of imperial unity and separatism, relations with the United States, and the advantages of federation in British North America.

I   THE VALUE OF COLONIES

1. Colonial Commerce

One of the major issues in the contemporary debate on colonies concerned the volume and value of colonial trade when compared with Britain's trade with foreign countries, and the relationship between commerce and political control of colonies. As an ardent advocate of empire, the *Colonial Gazette* in 1839 strongly emphasized the commercial advantages of overseas possessions.

. . .the Colonial trade of this country is, next to the home trade, the most valuable branch of its commerce,—giving employment exclusively to British shipping, and putting into activity a greater amount of British labour, in proportion to its extent, than any other part of our trade. It is an important, and, to us, a gratifying fact, that of 388,308 vessels of all flags—British and Foreign, having an aggregate burden of 62,109,462 tons, that entered and quitted the ports of the United Kingdom in the ten years from 1828 to 1837, the large proportion of 109,273 ships of 20,875,712 tons were employed in the Colonial trade, being 28 per cent of the number of ships, and 33½ per cent of the amount of tonnage:—in other words, one-third of the export and import trade of the United Kingdom is maintained with her Colonies and dependencies. This part of our trade, too, unlike that maintained with foreign countries, is not liable to violent fluctuations, nor to the uncertainties arising from rivalry or from political differences; but is steadily and constantly increasing from year to year. . . .

If we look to the value of British products and manufactures exported in the same period, we find, that while the whole foreign and colonial trade of the kingdom amounted to £408,670,046, the proportion sent to the British Colonies amounted to £111,993,953, or 27½ per cent of the whole. There is this further advantage attending the exports to our Colonies, that more than nine-tenths of the value is made up of goods which have received the last processes of manufacture; while our trade with the Continent of Europe is chiefly composed of raw products, such as coal, iron, lead, and salt, or of goods, such as cotton and linen yarn, which have been subjected to little beyond the initiating processes to fit them for use by foreign manufacturers, by whom they are converted into goods, which not only supply their home demand, but meet and compete with our manufacturers in their markets. . . .

What country in the world, either ancient or modern, could ever exhibit such a proof of Colonial greatness? Our possessions in North America, the West Indies, Australasia, the Mauritius, and the Cape of Good Hope, collectively contain populations amounting to 2,300,000 souls; and in 1837 they took from us manufactured goods to the value of £7,350,000, or more than £3 per head,—while our next best customers, the citizens of the United States, including their slave population, were customers to the value of only 7s.6d. each, or less than one-eighth of the amount purchased by each of our Colonial fellow-subjects. (*Colonial Gazette*, 2 March 1839)

A Tory newspaper, the *Morning Post*, reinforced this point of view when it argued in 1849 that once colonies became politically independent they were no longer prepared to offer Britain such favourable commercial terms. Anglo-American relations of that time seemed to provide evidence to support this contention.

. . . As to Canada, when we think of the difference of race and of hereditary sentiment—when we consider the facts of the history of the French portion of the colony, we see that it is contradictory to reason and experience to suppose the colony will voluntarily adopt the manners and become affected by the same wants and desires as the mother country. For look at the United States. The population there are of our own race, speak our language, inherit our energy, use our ancient laws, and in short have our manners and wants with far more similarity than we can ever expect to see in Canada. But do *they* fall into that "reciprocal trade" which the hon. and learned member for Sheffield [J. A. Roebuck, a radical M.P.] counts upon as a certainty? We levy no duty upon their wheat, but they levy eight shillings a quarter upon ours. We levy no duty upon their manufactured flour, but upon our manufactured goods they levy from twenty to forty per cent, and threaten to levy more. What nonsense, then, of the hon. and learned gentleman to assume that if we leave our colonies perfectly free and untrammelled, they will adopt a system of perfect reciprocity! There is no reason to expect any such thing. Experience is altogether against such an expectation. The *Liberal* confidence on this subject is but the confidence of a wild dream, begotten of self-conceit and the bigotry of a theoretic doctrine. . . .

We conceive it to be a gross error and delusion that our colonies can be of no advantage to us as colonies, and that if they were thriving communities with which we could drive a trade, we were better without them than with them. This is merely a short-sighted mercantile view. . . . It is not true that we can command a trade with independent countries as we can with our own colonies, and if it were, still there are other things besides trade to be considered. It is true that our trade with the United States of America is much more extensive now than it was when those states were British provinces. But we have only the trade, whereas in former times the whole wealth of those provinces and the provinces themselves were part of the wealth of the British empire. . . . Our trade with the

United States is great, so long as we are at peace, but we are not always at peace. Nations have other relations with each other than those of trade. Since we lost our extensive American possessions in the last century, there have been periods when all their strength was exerted for our destruction. . . . That time may come again. As it is, those provinces which once were a part of our empire are now our great rivals in the maritime world, and may yet wrest from us that naval superiority upon which our national greatness depends, and which forms our security against foreign violence and plunder. . . . (*Morning Post*, 28 May 1849)

Other commentators, however, were sceptical of the commercial value of colonies. J. R. McCulloch, like many other contemporary economists, believed that the cheapness and competitiveness of British goods made the possession of colonies unnecessary. He also appealed to the American example to support his point of view.

. . . Were this the proper place for entering upon such inquiries, it might be very easily shown that the advantages supposed peculiarly to belong to the colony trade, are in a great degree imaginary. No considerable colony will ever import any material quantity of goods from the mother-country, unless they be, at the same time, the cheapest and most suitable for her markets; and if they have this quality, the chances are ten to one that the colony would continue to import them were she to become independent. It is not by dint of custom-house regulations, but exclusively through the agency of comparatively cheap goods, that all great markets are acquired in the first instance, and are subsequently preserved. . . . And were any competitor to come into the field capable of supplying the Canadians with woollens, cottons, or hardware, on lower terms than we can supply them, we should be effectually shut out of their markets. It is not, therefore, to the fact of a country being a colony that we are to ascribe the circumstance of our carrying on a great *free* trade with it; but to the fact of our being able to supply it, or of its being able to supply us, with one or more articles or products in considerable demand on cheaper terms than it or they can be supplied from any other quarter. And a circumstance of this sort would, in most cases, lay the foundations of as extensive a trade with an independent state as with a colony. . . .

A country which founds a colony on the liberal principle of

allowing it to trade freely with all the world, necessarily possesses considerable advantages in its markets, from identity of language, religion, customs, &c. These are natural and legitimate sources of preference, of which it cannot be deprived; and these, combined with equal or greater cheapness of the products suitable for the colonial markets, will give its merchants the complete command of them. But all attempts at forcing a trade with colonies are sure to be pernicious alike to the mother-country and the colony; and make that intercourse a source of poverty and ill-will, which, if let alone, would be a source of reciprocal advantage. . . .

The American war seems to have decided, in as far as experience can decide anything, the question in regard to the policy of retaining colonies in a state of dependency that are determined to govern themselves. No colonies were ever regarded as half so valuable as those which now form the republic of the United States; and it was generally supposed that their emancipation would be decisive of the fate of England, that her sun would then set, and for ever! But have we really lost anything by that event? Has our trade, our wealth, or our power been in any degree impaired by the independence of the United States? The reverse is distinctly the case . . . notwithstanding its independence we have continued, and will continue in time to come, to reap all the advantage we can reasonably claim as the founders of this mighty empire in the wilderness. Englishmen will necessarily always command a preference in the American markets. And while we are disencumbered of the impossible task and enormous expenses attending the government and defence of all but boundless territories 3,000 miles distant, our intercourse with them grows with their growth; and we are as much benefited and enriched by them as we should have been had they continued in the same state of dependence as Malta or the Cape of Good Hope. . . . (J. R. McCulloch, *A Descriptive and Statistical Account of the British Empire*, London 1847, pp. 527-8, 531)

2. Protection or Free Trade?

In the discussion concerning the most profitable and effective means of conducting Britain's trading relations with overseas territories, Englishmen debated whether the country's commercial interests could best be promoted by the retention, reduction, or abolition of protective tariffs. From the time of American independence, minor alterations were made in the provisions of the Navigation Acts, which had governed the commercial relations of the empire since the seventeenth century. Major legislative changes, however, occurred in the 1820's when the reforms of Frederick Robinson and William Huskisson substantially modified the old principles of protection and monopoly, and substituted for them preferential duties for colonial over foreign goods and reciprocity with countries that granted Britain equivalent concessions. The reasons for these changes were explained by Huskisson in a parliamentary speech in 1825.

. . . It must be well known to every gentleman who hears me, that the long-established policy of all the European powers possessing colonies in the New World, and of this country among the rest, was that of an entire and rigid exclusion of those colonies from all commercial intercourse, except with the mother country. To uphold this exclusion, and to forbid all such intercourse, seemed of the very essence of colonization. . . . But if this has been the long-established basis of the colonial system, need I state the vast inroads which have been made upon this system within the last fifteen years? . . . Considering this almost general revolution in the system of colonial commerce—considering the influence of such a revolution upon the commerce of our own colonies, upon the commerce of rival nations, upon the views, and feelings, and speculations, of the mercantile part of the community, and of our own colonial population, is it not enough, of itself, to warrant, at least, the inquiry, whether so great a change in all around us does not call for some change on our part? . . .

. . . Have the colonies, of which the trade has been thrown open, benefited by this enlargement of their intercourse? Are they likely to benefit still more? Rivals in the same productions, competitors in the same markets, can we, in the long-run, with our system of monopoly, stand against their freedom of trade? If we cannot, are we not risking the good-will and attachment of our colonies, as well as the interests of our commerce? Is perseverance in such a system, politically wise, or practically safe? Is the great change, begun half a century ago, and still in progress, in the political and commercial state of the vast continent of America, from the Gulph of St. Lawrence to Cape Horn, to lead to no change in our mode of administering the extensive possessions, both continental and insular, which remain under our dominion and protection in that quarter of the globe? Do the immense and rapidly growing commerce and navigation of the United States of America, suggest no matter for consideration, in reference to our own commercial and naval interests? . . .

. . . I would ask any man, whether . . . the disseverance of the United States from the British empire, viewed as a mere question of commerce, has been an injury to this country?—Whether their emancipation from the commercial thraldom of the colonial system has really been prejudicial to the trade and industry of Great Britain? If the answer must be, that it has not been prejudicial, is there no useful admonition to be derived from this example?—Contemplate the possibility of another set of provinces, emancipated from commercial thraldom, but firmly maintaining their political connexion —their commercial marine a part of our commercial marine—their seamen a part of our seamen—their population a part of our strength.—Consider whether it be not worth while to attempt a course which promises, both to those provinces and to the mother country, all the commercial benefits of a free trade, together with all the political advantages of our continuing parts of one great empire, and enjoying alike, under the sway and protection of the same sovereign, all the rights and privileges of British subjects. . . .

From all the experience which we can collect from the conduct of this country, in respect to Ireland, and to its colonies,—from all that we witness of what is passing in the colonies of other states, I come clearly to this conclusion—that so far as the colonies themselves are concerned, their prosperity is cramped and impeded by the old system of exclusion and monopoly; and I feel myself equally warranted in my next inference, that whatever tends to increase the prosperity of the colonies, cannot fail, in the long run, to advance, in an equal degree, the general interests of the parent state. . . .

There can, therefore, be no doubt that it would be expedient to permit the same latitude of trade to the ships of other countries, as is now allowed to those of the United States. But I go further; I am prepared to open the commerce of our colonies to all friendly states, upon the same principle (though of course with some difference in the detail of its modifications), upon which they are at liberty to trade with Jersey, or with Ireland. With the exception of some articles . . . I propose to admit a free intercourse between all our colonies and other countries, either in British ships, or in the ships of those countries, allowing the latter to import all articles, the growth, produce, or manufacture of the country to which the ship belongs, and to export from such colonies all articles whatever of their growth, produce, or manufacture, either to the country from which such ship came, or to any other part of the world, the United Kingdom and all its dependencies excepted. All intercourse between the mother country and the colonies, whether direct or circuitous, and all intercourse of the colonies with each other, will be considered as a coasting trade to be reserved entirely and absolutely to ourselves. By this arrangement, the foundation of our navigation laws will be preserved, whilst the colonies will enjoy a free trade with foreign countries. . . . The importation of foreign goods into the colonies, I propose, should be made subject to moderate duties, but such as may be found sufficient for the fair protection of our own productions of the like nature. . . .

. . . an open trade, especially to a rich and thriving country, is infinitely more valuable than any monopoly, however exclusive, which the public power of the state may be able, either to enforce against its own colonial dominions, or to establish in its intercourse with other parts of the world. . . .

. . . I cannot doubt, that without any other encouragement than freedom of trade, and a lenient administration, these [Canadian] provinces will, henceforward, make the most rapid strides towards prosperity—that connecting their prosperity with the liberal treatment of the mother country, they will neither look with envy at the growth of other states on the same continent, nor wish for the dissolution of old and the formation of new political connexions. . . . (*Hansard*, New Series, XII, 21 March 1825, 1099-1100, 1104-5, 1111)

Although many leading economists and some politicians condemned the evils of protective tariffs, little headway was made towards the abolition of restrictions on colonial trade during the thirties and early forties. The victory of free trade in England, marked by the repeal of the corn laws in 1846, represented a triumph for Richard Cobden and the Manchester radicals, within and outside parliament. Arguments drawn from economic theory and practice were extensively employed during the debate preceding repeal, with both protectionists and their opponents examining the likely effects of free trade on colonial relations and the future of the empire. Contrasting views were presented in the course of debates in the House of Lords in May 1846

by Lord Stanley, a leading Tory spokesman, and Earl Grey, a Whig
advocate of free trade.

. . . Now, destroy this principal of protection, and I tell you in
this place that you destroy the whole basis upon which your Colonial
system rests. . . . It is by your Colonial system, based upon the
principles of protection, that you have extended your arms—I do
not mean your military arms, I mean your commercial arms—to
every quarter and to every corner of the globe. It is to your Colonial
system that you owe it that there is not a sea on which the flag of
England does not float; that there is not a quarter of the world in
which the language of England is not heard; that there is not a
quarter of the globe, that there is no zone in either hemisphere, in
which there are not thousands who recognize the sovereignty of
Britain—to whom that language and that flag speak of a home,
dear, though distant, of common interests, of common affections—
men who share in your glories—men who sympathize in your ad-
versities, men who are proud to bear their share of your burdens,
to be embraced within the arms of your commercial policy, and
to feel that they are members of your great and imperial Zollverein.
It was said, I think, by Mr. Cobden, that a system of protection is
a system of mutual robbery. I admit that it is "a mutual system";
it is a system under which, and in accordance with which, each
surrenders some advantage to himself, for the purpose of partaking
in the general advantage of all—it is a system by which each sacrifices something of the profits of his own trade for the purpose of
ensuring a reciprocal advantage from others . . . a system in which
both parties gain—both parties are secured against hostile interference—against foreign intrusion—against foreign caprice. . . .
Sure I am, that whatever disadvantage may be sustained by the
trifling additional amount of a protecting duty on articles of colonial
produce; and whatever may be the small amount added to the cost
on the British article under a protecting duty still the disadvantage
is amply compensated by the extension of our power over the wide
world—by securing for us in every quarter friends and allies—by
securing for our people certain employment and certainty of consumption, uninterfered with by foreign competition—and by em-
ploying a vast amount of British seamen, ready to act at any moment
in defence, and for the sustainment of the strength, of the Empire. . . .
I know that your political economists are for casting off your Colo-

nies, that they say let them trade with us, or any other country —give them the full advantages of free trade—let us not restrain them—as they are removed from all protection, let them also be free from all burdensome duty. I do not say that I have any doubt as to the loyalty of these Colonies, for I have no doubt of their attachment; but I do say that you should not do anything to weaken that attachment—that you should be very careful that, in granting commercial independence, you do not take a step to their political independence. You cannot tell them to trade freely with all nations, without also telling them to look no longer to you as their protectors. . . . (*Hansard*, 3rd Series, LXXXVI, 25 May 1846, 1165-7)

. . . The noble Lord [Stanley] produced a great impression on the House by describing the effect which this measure [repeal of the corn laws] would be likely to create upon the condition of our Colonies and upon our interests as connected with the maintenance of our colonial possessions. That was a subject of very great importance; and he (Earl Grey) was so impressed with the high value which ought to be laid on the preservation of our colonial empire, that he would admit that if this law would shake the security of that empire, or its connexion with the mother country, it would deserve the gravest consideration before that House should assent to it. He, however, entertained unhesitatingly the conviction that, so far from being a disadvantage to the Colonies—so far from having a tendency to weaken the ties which unite them to us, the adoption, in the largest sense, and in the most complete manner, of the principles of commercial freedom, was the policy, of all others, which was best calculated to strengthen those ties. His noble Friend had asked, if the colonists were told that they were no more to the country than Frenchmen or Dutchmen, what inducement they would have to wish to be united with this country? To that he (Earl Grey) would answer, that . . . it was not proposed to apply the principle of the removal of restriction to the Colonies exclusively, but it was intended to apply to them a principle which we proposed to apply to ourselves. Would any one say that Cumberland and Yorkshire would be treated badly by this measure, because we did not leave them a protecting duty? If our own counties, then, were to be treated in the same manner by this Bill as the Colonies, then the Colonies had no reason to complain. He could understand how some persons in the old country, where there was a great competition for employment, could be induced to take a shortsighted view of the subject, and thus he could perceive how it was that many persons had been induced to form the opinion that protection was an advantage, and that it was not wise to let in foreign goods to compete with our home market; but with respect to the Colonies there was no such difficulty as that competition for employment. On the contrary, in every one of our own Colonies, the great difficulty was to find sufficient labour to develop fully its natural resources; and if the effect of the proposed system should be to divert labour in the Colonies to its natural and most productive channels, instead of to artificial and unproductive channels, there could be no doubt that it would be an advantage to them. Could any one doubt that Canada was poorer now than she would have been if there never had been a protective duty in favour of her timber? If, instead of letting into our markets bad timber, when we could have had good, we had never adopted that system, Canada would be better off; and the same principle would apply to all our Colonies. The Colonies had received no advantage from protecting duties, whilst in many cases those duties had been directly injurious to them . . . and as regarded the effect of commercial dependence in strengthening the ties between the Colonies and this country, he would put it to their Lordships whether the system of commercial dependence had in reality strengthened the ties between the Colonies and the mother country. Did they not all know that jealousy, arising from that commercial dependence, had produced that American war which ended in the loss of those extensive Colonies to the Crown of this country? He . . . did not say that in the present state of importance those States would have been kept in dependence to the British Crown; but they might have parted from us in a different manner, and without leaving any feeling of jealousy towards the mother country, if it had not been for that commercial dependence. . . . For his part he believed that the connexion between the Colonies and the mother country was a mutual advantage, requiring no such support to maintain it. In our colonial empire we possessed friends and allies in every quarter of the globe . . . whilst they enjoyed the inestimable advantages of being an integral part of the most powerful, and most enlightened, and most civilized nation upon the face of the earth. They gloried—and he knew that they felt it as a glory—in calling themselves British subjects, and in having their interests and rights protected by the power of this country . . . he believed that if they pursued a liberal policy in other respects towards the Colonies, by extending to them the dearest right of Englishmen, the privilege of self-government, and not needlessly interfering in their domestic concerns—that if they adopted a sound policy, politically as well as commercially, they would bind them to us with chains which no power on earth could break; and the connexion between them and the Parent State would continue until they far exceeded ourselves in population. . . . (*Hansard*, 3rd Series, LXXXVI, 28 May 1846, 1307-10)

When free trade became the avowed policy of the British government in 1846, there was considerable debate amongst interested parties over the effects of such a policy on Canada's economic and political position. The matter was complicated by the fact that in 1843 the Tory ministry had given wheat and flour exported from Canada, whether originating there or in the United States, a favourable preference in the British market. The sudden removal of this preference three years later meant that considerable colonial investment in the corn trade and Canadian hopes of profit were now threatened by effective American competition. Nevertheless, the *Globe*, a liberal, free-trade paper, emphasized the advantages of free trade for British North America and denounced as impolitic the final gesture of protection in 1843.

. . . Canada *has* a protective grievance; and a very substantial one—the most presentable, indeed, of any on the list of those now daily urged, in some shape, upon the attention of the public at home. . . . Canada is not, naturally, a corn-exporting country. It does not, on an average, grow more than it consumes—hardly so much. But when Lord STANLEY'S bill passed [in 1843], it was accepted as the basis of a guaranteed corn trade between England and the United States, through Canada. The colonists made arrangements accordingly: built wharfs, warehouses, and mills along the borders of the lakes, and poured all the capital they could spare, or raise, into the new trade. In the autumn of 1845 came the first signs of approaching scarcity in the United Kingdom—the Corn-laws were assailed, and, as we all know, given up; and the Act of 1843 went down with the new scale of the preceding year; leaving the Canadians to do the best they could with their useless investments for the transit and grinding trade thus snatched out of their fingers. Here they may fairly complain; but only of the last act of the Protectionist policy. An earlier triumph of sound principles would have spared them the infliction; and they need apprehend nothing of a similar description from a government acting, as all future governments of the country must act, upon the principles of free trade.

Thus the prevailing depression which, operating coincidently with the withdrawal of protection, has brought up cries of distress and discontent from all our colonial dependencies, more or less, has also had a similar effect in Canada—not because Canada has yet suffered materially from the loss of protection, but because she especially writhes under the ruinous consequences of a last luckless effort of the Protectionists to maintain their policy, and has at the same time to bear with the inevitable results of a severe commercial crisis, crippling the resources of her chief customers in this country. It need hardly be observed that no subsequent *political* circumstances could be reasonably expected to avert discontent in a community so situated as to its material interests. (*Globe*, 17 August 1849)

The *Morning Post* in 1849, however, strongly condemned the adoption of free trade as the basis of Anglo-Canadian trading relations, since it meant commercial ruin for Canada and might foster colonial disaffection.

There are not many who fairly estimate the trial to which the loyalty of British Canadians is subject by the pernicious system of policy which the mother country has pursued for some years past. Much as agricultural producers in England feel the injurious effects of a policy which subjects their industry to the crushing influence of unchecked foreign competition, that policy is found still more galling in a British province which depends mainly upon the export of grain, and which export is thwarted by a foreign policy [American tariff protection] directly the opposite of that which the British Government has adopted. The wheat-grower of Upper Canada is no longer allowed any favour or preference in the British market. The American grower, who has easier access to British markets than the Canadian grower has, comes to the Mersey or the Thames with his cargo, which is as freely admitted as if it were of British growth. The Canadian would gladly, in his turn, supply the markets of the northern States of America, but he asks in vain to be admitted to those markets on the same terms as the American grower is admitted to British markets. . . .

We cannot conceive a greater blindness of political bigotry than that which perseveres in handing over advantage after advantage, and privilege after privilege, to foreign countries, without stipulating for anything in return. The Canadians find ruin on every side. On the side of Great Britain they are virtually excluded by a law which makes the Americans legally equal, while naturally they have a superiority. On the side of America they are excluded by a law which gives a legal superiority to the citizens and producers of the United States, and neutralises the natural advantages of the Canadians.

How are the Canadians to escape from this doubly disadvantageous position? There are two ways. One is in a retracing of the steps which the Legislature of Great Britain has taken, under the impulse of the blind bigotry and stupid theorising of the Manchester school. The other is by the Canadians abandoning or throwing off the Government of Great Britain, and "annexing" their country to the Republic of the United States. The Republican Government would protect them. It would give them all the markets of the United States to sell their agricultural produce in, and it would exclude foreign competition so far as an eight shilling duty would exclude it.

. . . If, then, they have no hope of the injurious British law being repealed, who can wonder that a sense of self-preservation should turn them towards America? The duty of allegiance is indeed no light thing, but allegiance on the one hand implies . . . protection on the other. If the British Government will not give protection, it is sheer tyranny to extort allegiance. . . . (*Morning Post,* 15 May 1849)

The last symbolic vestige of the old colonial system was removed in 1849 with the repeal of the Navigation Laws. Many supporters of abolition argued that this would ease the commercial crisis in British North America because the St. Lawrence would then be open to the ships and trade of all nations. This optimistic view was presented by the *Morning Chronicle,* a ministerial Whig newspaper.

. . . Canada is in a singular, and, in some respects, in an anomalous position, as regards her relations with the mother country; and it is her interest, even more than ours, to have the anomalies removed. She possesses entire political freedom; "responsible government" has been irrevocably conceded to her; her domestic legislation is unfettered. . . . But it would be an error to imagine that the theory of non-interference has been consistently carried out, and that Great Britain and Canada have altogether ceased to impose on each other those burdens which formed the essence of our vicious "colonial system". Even in Canada, several incidents of that system yet remain, and, in every case, they are productive of unmixed evil . . . chiefly, we fetter her trade by our Navigation-laws.

. . . It is not surprising, that, to British colonists, there should appear a strong *prima facie* objection to free trade; for we have, of late years, shown them exclusively the bright side of Protection, by making it a pretext for paying an annual tribute into their pockets; and it requires much foresight and reflection to discern the latent injury inflicted, by such an artificial system, under the guise of favour and support. Even, therefore, where the merits of any particular question, connected with freedom of commerce, are perfectly clear, there is, in the minds of a large party in each colony, a disinclination to admit them, for fear of sanctioning a principle which British colonists have been taught to dread. Such is the case with respect to the Navigation-laws in Canada . . . for, as regards the injury inflicted, by the existing restrictions, on the commerce of the colony, there could be but one opinion, if the matter were considered without bias or prejudice. The question, in fact, is nothing less than whether the whole carrying-trade of North-Western America shall belong to the Canadians, or to the Americans. The vast increase, within the last two years, of the provision-trade between America and Europe, has led to a corresponding increase of production in Western Canada, and in the North-Western States of the Union— and, consequently, to increased competition between the Canadian and American "forwarders", for a monopoly of the carrying-trade. The advantages of the two routes are so nearly balanced as to make a very small matter turn the scale. Before the repeal of the Corn-laws, in 1846, the Canadians possessed, by means of the differential duty, an advantage in the British market, which enabled them, on the whole, to overcome, or, at least, to hold their ground against, their rivals. With a view to the maintenance of this advantage, the Provincial Government borrowed a large sum of money from the Imperial

Treasury, which it invested chiefly in improving the navigation of the St. Lawrence. . . . Within the last two years, however, there has been a decided falling off in the Canadian carrying-trade. The Erie Canal and the Hudson have been competing successfully with the St. Lawrence. . . . The chief benefit, accordingly, of the money and labour already expended on the St. Lawrence, is in danger of being thrown away, unless means can be found of cheapening the ocean freight from the port of shipment. Of such means the most obvious is, the throwing open of the St. Lawrence to the ships of all nations, and thus reducing, by competition, the price of freights. Accordingly, the general feeling in the province, with the exception of those interested in ship-building, and of those who fear and detest free trade generally (without knowing why), is now in favour of the alteration. . . . (*Morning Chronicle*, 14 December 1848)

The *Standard*, a Tory newspaper, was sceptical whether Canada would gain any advantages from the repeal of the Navigation Laws at a time of commercial depression.

. . . The Canadians . . . are now bent upon the repeal of our Navigation Laws, as a compensation for the injury they have sustained in the withdrawal of protection from their timber and corn trades. . . .
It would be easy to lay before the Canadians demonstrative proofs that a repeal of our navigation laws would do them no possible good; that facilities of navigation, even supposing the repeal to afford such facilities to any sensible extent, which it would not, must be useless to a people stripped of their trade, in a state of bankruptcy, with wharves unoccupied, and without one single craft from beyond the sea. . . . But though it would be easy to lay the proof before the Canadians, they know little of human nature who fancy that it would be easy, or even possible, to convince them. Yet, if they only looked to what is passing in the next neighbouring country they would see the true foundation of commercial prosperity. Navigation, like every other department of industry, is protected in the United States. It is true that, misled by our example, some American statesmen lately made an approach, though a cautious one, to free-trade principles; but they are now retracing their steps with the precipitation of fear. . . . (*Standard*, 20 September 1848)

3. The Expense of Colonies

Much of the contemporary debate concerning the value of colonies centred on the substantial cost to the British exchequer and taxpayer of colonial administration and defence. Reduction of the current volume of imperial expenditure was persistently demanded by Englishmen of almost every shade of political persuasion, but it was difficult to reconcile the successful pursuit of economy with the maintenance of a far-flung empire. For this reason, even the supporters of empire felt it necessary to urge that financial burdens should be transferred as soon as possible to the shoulders of the colonists. Part of the difficulty for English critics was that colonial expenditure remained an unfathomable item hidden in annual British budgets, as the *Morning Chronicle* pointed out in 1849, and neither politicians nor the public could completely disentangle its ramifications.

. . . To analyse and dissect the various financial Returns, comprising the details of the public expenditure, for the purpose of ascertaining the net cost of maintaining and administering our widely scattered possessions, is a task which might well baffle the most persevering student of official statistics. So multifarious are the charges, so diffused over a large surface of accounts, so mixed up and complicated with other heads and items of expenditure, that it is next to impossible for any man to pronounce, after the most careful investigation of the different statements and estimates, how much the Colonies actually cost Great Britain, or what would be the saving to her from their manumission. The Parliamentary Returns, which profess to furnish the desired information in a compendious form, afford, as is manifest on the face of them, an extremely vague and inadequate representation of the facts. We have now before us an abstract . . . which professes to comprise the total colonial expenditure of Great Britain in the year 1846-7. According to this paper, the military expenditure amounted to £2,928,069; the naval to £82,395; and the net civil expenditure to £492,192: total cost to Great Britain, £3,500,472. According to a similar return for 1834-5, we find that the charge for that year was, under the first head, £1,924,337; under the second, £42,322; under the third, £434,161; and for the total, £2,431,900. The rate of increase in our admitted colonial expenditure would, therefore, appear to be somewhat rapid. . . .

It is of course superfluous to observe, that the sum above stated as the net cost to Great Britain of keeping her colonies in leading strings . . . is a very different thing from the actual dead loss to the mother-country which results from her present method of administration. The payments that she is called upon to make for extraordinary emergencies—the surcharges which arise every now and then when a rebellion or disturbance breaks out, which the parental authority steps in to put down—when a troublesome young settlement gets to loggerheads with its neighbours, or turns restive against the dictation of Downing-street—all such supernumerary disbursements, which, on an average of years, form a heavy item in the Imperial Balance-sheet, are passed over *sub silentio* in the official computation. And if we add to the cost of suppressing the ebullitions, which misgovernment or interference have provoked, the indirect loss occasioned by a policy which stunts the natural growth of the colonies themselves, as much as it damps and discourages the spirit of colonization at home, we shall find it difficult to estimate, even in a pecuniary point of view, the injury we inflict on ourselves by deferring the concession which must inevitably be made, sooner or later, of a just and reasonable freedom to our dependencies. (*Morning Chronicle*, 27 December 1849)

Britain's expenditure on colonies fell into three broad categories: contributions to civil administrations overseas, military expenditure including army, navy, ordnance, and commissariat expenses, and support for the clergy of the Church of England. Discussion of imperial expenditure on civil establishments in British North America can be aptly illustrated by the comments of Joseph Hume, a radical politician and the most tireless advocate of economy, and Robert Wilmot Horton, the Tory parliamentary under-secretary at the Colonial Office, made in a parliamentary debate in 1824.

Mr. *Hume* said, that Upper Canada was only separated by an ideal line from the colonies of the United States, which not only paid the whole expenses of their civil, but their military establishments. It was extremely unfair and unjust, that the people of England should be called upon to pay the expenses of the civil as well as the military establishments of her colonies. Before the people of England were taxed, for the purpose of maintaining a civil establishment in Upper Canada, it was fitting that at least they should know of what that establishment consisted. It appeared to him a most improper appropriation of the public money. The people of Canada should provide for their own establishments. If all the officers who were kept there were useful, let their maintenance be provided for by the legislative assembly; but if, as he believed, they were considered unnecessary, why then let them at once be discharged. But, he believed, the people of Canada would throw upon the shoulders of the people of England, all these burthens (and naturally enough too), if the people of England were weak enough to submit to it. . . .

Mr. *Wilmot Horton* said, that. . . . Up to the year 1816, all the expenses of that colony were borne by this country. . . . Now two-thirds of the expenses were raised by the colony itself. The aggregate expenditure amount to £30,000, of which sum £20,000 were furnished by the colony; and he thought it would be unjust in their present condition to call upon them to supply more. . . . The question which the House had to look at, was the total expense of the civil establishment of Upper Canada, viewed in relation to her resources and the necessity of maintaining a local government. Now, was the general expense of the colony more than should be borne? Was it more than the mother country should contribute to a colony, as yet in an infant state? The hon. member had asked, what advantage we derived from this colony? . . . It was difficult to estimate the value which the country derived from her colonies. The hon. member for Aberdeen [Hume] seemed to think that there could be no advantages produced, unless they could be shewn to him arithmetically on a balance sheet. But, in speaking of our colonial system, he always felt that he was speaking of the wealth, the power, and the commercial resources of the empire; and he was persuaded that, enlightened as the country now was by sound and rational principles of political science, the nation would be able to appreciate her colonial advantages, even though their precise pecuniary value could not be demonstrated on a balance sheet. . . . (*Hansard*, New Series, X, 12 March 1824, 955-8)

British expenditure on civil establishments in North America was gradually reduced during the thirties and forties as the colonists assumed increased responsibility for the administration of their own internal affairs. Meanwhile the British government also contributed towards the salaries of Anglican clergymen in Canada. The religious and financial considerations raised by this support were debated in

April 1829 when it was proposed to grant £16,182 to the Society for the Propagation of the Gospel, which handled imperial financial grants to the Church of England in the colonies. Again Hume was a leading critic, and other speakers included Sir George Murray, the Tory colonial secretary, and William Trant, a minor Tory politician. Largely as a result of parliamentary criticism, the Whig government, which came into office in 1830, soon discontinued support for the ecclesiastical establishments in British North America.

Mr. *Hume* said, he could not permit that opportunity to pass without protesting against the grant. The principle of it was highly objectionable; for it set one class of the community in array against the other, on religious grounds: it created discord, by giving to the members of a favoured religion, a monopoly of the public money. This undue patronage by government—this engrossment of parliamentary grants—was contrary to the principles of Christianity, which inculcated peace and good will to all men, instead of generating, as this grant did, discord and disunion. From 1814 to 1827 not less than £158,000 of the public money had been expended by the Society for the Propagation of the Gospel in Foreign Parts, chiefly in Canada and the North American colonies; but the public had yet to learn the benefits of this large expenditure. The House would scarcely believe the small proportion which the members of the religion of that Society, bore to those of the other denominations in those colonies. Nova Scotia he would take for an example; for the church establishment of which £11,482 was annually voted by that House; and yet, so little influence did that church possess over the inhabitants of that colony, that the sum of their contributions to the church of England was only £1,024. The population of that colony, exclusive of Cape Breton, was one hundred and twenty-three thousand eight hundred. Of these but twenty-eight thousand six hundred were members of the church of England, while the members of the church of Scotland were thirty-seven thousand; and yet, for the former the people of England were called upon annually to pay £11,482 while for the latter church, which had the more numerous congregation, parliament, in its munificence granted but £75 a-year. There were twenty thousand Catholics, nine thousand baptists, and twenty-five thousand Methodists; the remainder of the population being Dissenters of other denominations. He thought it was not wonderful that those other sects should view with a jealous eye a church so favoured, and that discord and disunion should be the consequences. The withholding that grant, then, would not only induce a state of things more in harmony with the pacific state of the Gospel, but it would be a considerable saving of the public money. . . .

Sir G. *Murray* said, that the hon. member had stated, very truly, the sentiments which he had expressed on a recent occasion; namely, that he deprecated nothing more than the introduction into the new world of those religious differences which unhappily had too long prevailed in the old. . . . But he conceived that the vote now before the House was intimately connected, not with the interest of one sect, or of one religion, but with the interest of religion in general; and that interest, he conceived, would be materially injured by withholding this grant. The hon. gentleman must be aware, that amongst those persons who left this country, and were progressively settling in America, there were a great variety of sects; and, situated as those settlers were, every man's imagination was apt to go to work to devise some mode of worship for himself, which was calculated to produce a state of things extremely detrimental, both to himself and to the state at large; and therefore he thought it was right, on the part of the church, to send certain competent persons into those provinces to prevent such an evil. . . .

Mr. *Trant* supported the original motion, and expressed his intention of watching narrowly the motion of the hon. member for Aberdeen, on the subject of the colonies, because he thought he perceived a disposition to discourage the progress of the church of England in the colonies. Now, he would maintain that it was right they should uphold the church of England in the British colonies; and therefore he could not agree in the doctrines laid down by the hon. member. He would not consent to any proposition which tended to check the progress of the established church in any part of our possessions. . . . (*Hansard*, New Series, XXI, 6 April 1829, 455-60)

The cost of defending British possessions overseas entailed substantial expenditure on fortifications, garrisons, barracks, and ordnance. The volume and purpose of this expenditure on military establishments in British North America were widely debated, especially since many Englishmen felt that this expense was conclusive proof of colonial misgovernment, and that British possessions in that quarter could not be successfully defended against the ambitions of the United States if the willing loyalty of the inhabitants was not secured. Many of the relevant issues were raised during the course of a parliamentary debate in 1829 on the fortification of Kingston and Halifax. The speakers included John Maberley, a radical, Maurice Fitzgerald, a Tory advocate of empire, Henry Labouchere, a moderate radical, Lord Howick, a young Whig with some radical sympathies at this time and who in 1830 was appointed parliamentary under-secretary at the Colonial Office, William Huskisson, a Tory reformer, and Sir Robert Peel, the Tory home secretary.

Mr. *Maberley* said . . . there was no certainty of our being able to hold Canada. When these works were established, the colonists might take it into their heads to say, "We are not satisfied with your government; we wish to govern ourselves". Thus the country would have had the expense of establishing the works to no purpose. But, he would ask, of what benefit was Canada to us, in a commercial point of view? He would say that, instead of a benefit, it was a disadvantage. . . .

Mr. *M. Fitzgerald* complained of the practice of treating the question of the colonies as a matter of pounds, shillings and pence. If parliament was determined to have colonies, it was their duty to preserve them. Halifax was one of the finest harbours in the world, and as long as we held it, and had a canal to carry up stores into the interior, the Americans would never again venture to attack us upon Lake Ontario, or disturb that commerce which we carried on with the inhabitants of the distant settlements. Looking, therefore, at the importance of preserving Canada, and the importance of being provided with a proper defence in the event of war, he felt bound to support the grant.

Mr. *Labouchere* said, that no person was more certain than he was, that it was impossible to keep Canada without possessing the entire and cordial affections of the inhabitants; and while those affections were devoted to this country in the manner they had been, he would be the last man in that House to consent to abandon the country or the people. In the event of a war with America—which, though he did not think probable, he was bound to view as possible—it would be found that they had laid out the money now called for most economically. He wished this country to remain on friendly terms with the United States, and therefore he thought it unwise to hazard that friendship, by leaving Canada a tempting object for invasion. He should support not only the present, but all future votes, of the like nature. This country would not be acting fairly and justly to Canada, if protection were not extended to her; and when he spoke of protection, he meant effectual protection. When he said he would vote for the present and for future grants of the same nature, he gave that pledge with this condition—that efforts should be made, and made immediately, to give to Canada a wise, an efficient, and a conciliatory government; and that a complete change should be made in the system of disorder and misrule which had too long prevailed there. . . .

Lord *Howick* said, that . . . all our foreign colonies would in the lapse of time, become independent of the mother country. That such an event must happen there was no denying; and consequently this country ought in time to prepare for the separation, not by fortifying the Canadas, but by preparing them to become independent. With this view, instead of hurrying the present vote through the House, let ministers come down next session with a statement of such reasonable expenditure as would be required for the furtherance of a measure which sooner or later must take place.

Mr. *Huskisson* said, that. . . . He could not agree that the United States were not ambitious of possessing new territories; and of all the British settlements, he felt assured that the Canadas formed the first object of their ambition. He believed that the ambition which prompted America, in 1812, was ready to be called into action, on the first occasion. The House should recollect, that but for the defenceless state of the Canadas in 1812, that aggression which cost this country so much of its best blood and treasure, would never have taken place. Were we not wise, therefore, to provide against a similar aggression, by adopting those precautions which sound policy dictated? . . . The question was this—shall England provide against future aggression in the Canadas, by rendering them capable of defence, or shall we give them up at once, with the loss of national character and honour, and overlooking those sacred duties which, as a parent country, we owed to a tried and faithful people. If we determined, as it became our station in the rank of nations to do, to defend the Canadas, we ought, in the first place, to consider whether that defence should be undertaken with every fair prospect of success, or whether we should, by a niggard vote at present, not only render that success doubtful, but increase the expense which it would cost us at least tenfold? . . . he would say, let the Canadas be ours as long as we are in a situation to retain them, and as long as their loyal people shall claim our protection; and if, in the course of time,—as who shall say that our connexion shall be eternal?—a separation shall take place, let the country to which we were once united, and from which we parted with regret, be one to which, in our mutual necessity, we may look forward to each other for support and assistance. . . .

Mr. Secretary *Peel* said . . . was it not wise, in time of peace, to make preparation for an effectual defence? The hon. gentleman himself must admit, unless he was prepared to recommend the abandoning of the Canadas—that the most economical mode was, to assist the physical strength of the population, by some system of fortification.—But, he would ask, could this country abandon its Colonies? . . . He begged the House to consider what would be the effect produced on the other Colonies, if this country were to abandon the Canadas. If they saw the mighty power of this country shrinking into narrow dimensions, and exerted only for selfish purposes, what conclusion must they form? He had often seen with regret a disposition shewn to under-rate the value of our possessions abroad. He should be sorry to see this country, on any course of abstract reasoning or political philosophy, make the experiment of trying the effect the loss of the Colonies would have on the strength of the empire. . . . Was it, then, for the honour of Great Britain to signify to her Colonies, that she was about to abandon them as a burdensome connection? Was she to tell them that, on account of the danger of their being attacked, their defence would be too onerous for her, and that therefore she purposed to dissolve the union? . . . If ever they did form an independent government, God grant the dissolution of the connection might be an amicable one! But he contended that, looking forward to the time when they might amicably separate from us, it was by no means certain, that this money to provide them with adequate means of defence would be ill expended. (*Hansard*, New Series, XIX, 7 July 1828, 1630-32, 1635-40)

Both critics and supporters of empire were aware that so long as Britain possessed colonies they had to be defended. Tory imperialists considered this form of military expenditure desirable as well as essential, and for them demands for economy were shortsighted and likely to be disastrous. Typical of this minority point of view were the comments of the *Naval and Military Gazette* in 1838.

. . . The recent events in Canada have naturally engrossed the consideration of every man throughout the empire, and will, doubtless, fully demonstrate the folly of allowing Government to be under the dictation of pseudo patriots, whose eternal cry is "economy". No Ministry, in which a sufficient confidence is not reposed for the just and judicious appropriation of public monies, can possibly govern a nation like Great Britain, whose policy must be diffuse—whose colonies are illumined by a never-setting sun. This idol of patriotic pretence, "economy", must give way to "judicious expenditure", if we desire to maintain that dignified station in which England has been placed by her Army and Navy. Our colonies must be preserved at any cost, however cavilled at by interested declaimers (of very doubtful patriotism), under the false cry of "expense"; and who thus gain a notoriety which may prove, eventually, fatal to them. Colonies to Great Britain are as essential as Fleets and Armies, not only as emblems of greatness, but, moreover, as drains for the surplus population of the country, and, at the same time, as sources for the consumption of her manufactures. But the *supremacy* of England is vitally dependent upon her possession of distant colonies, if as *nurseries only* for her seamen; for a deficiency of sailors (and all blue jackets are not sailors) in the Naval branch of her armament would unequivocally lead to a diminution of her wealth, strength, and importance—nay, to her very existence as an independent nation, let alone her station as mistress of the world. Her colonies, then, must be preserved—their imports from the mother-country will amply repay the cost incurred. But England must no longer play the stepmother, and starve her bantling, in the idolatrous pursuit of economy, to gain the deceptive smiles of traitors, rebels, or even *patriots*, as certain brawlers designate themselves. The mere acknowledgment of the connexion between the mother-country and her distant relatives will not be sufficient;—the niggard policy of England must be exchanged for a liberal system of encouragement, long due to, but studiously withheld from, not only the colonies, but from the Army and from the Navy, each of which have been unfeelingly exposed to neglect, which calls loudly for redress. . . . (*Naval and Military Gazette*, 10 November 1838)

Critics of empire, on the other hand, referred to the volume of military expenditure as a convincing argument for getting rid of the colonies. Richard Cobden, as a free trader and Manchester radical, was often cited as an exponent of this point of view, but, as the following extract suggests, his emphasis was sometimes placed on the reform of imperial relations rather than on unequivocal separation.

. . . We are told we must keep up enormous armaments, because we have got so many colonies. People tell me I want to abandon our colonies; but I say, do you intend to hold your colonies by the sword, by armies, and ships of war? That is not a permanent hold upon them. I want to retain them by their affections. If you tell me that our soldiers are kept for their police, I answer, the English people cannot afford to pay for their police. The inhabitants of those colonies are a great deal better off than the mass of the people of England —they are in the possession of a vast deal more of the comforts of life than the bulk of those paying taxes here. . . . Our colonies are very able to protect themselves. . . . With regard to our navy, they tell us it is necessary because of our trade with the colonies. I should have thought it was just that trade which wanted no navy at all. It is a sort of coasting trade; our ships are at home when they get to our colonies. We don't want any navy to protect our trade with America, which is a colony emancipated. . . . (Cobden's speech in Manchester, 10 January 1849, as quoted in J. Bright and J. E. T. Rogers, eds., *Speeches on Questions of Public Policy by Richard Cobden*, London 1870, II, 485-6)

There was much truth in the argument that local self-government would be the cheapest and most effective means of providing for imperial defence, since the colonists would then possess a freedom which they would be prepared to defend at their own expense. Even advocates of empire like Lord Howick, who became the Third Earl Grey in 1845, were anxious to reduce imperial expenditure on military establishments overseas by shifting the financial burden on to the colonists.

. . . It is impossible to disguise from oneself that there is a growing impatience as to the amount of expense they [the colonies] occasion, & a strong feeling that they ought during peace to pay for their own Military expenditure, nor can I deny that there is some Justice in this & that by degrees they ought to be called upon to do more for themselves—To proceed indeed as Cobden & his friends w[oul]d wish w[oul]d be to abandon the Greater part at all Events of our Colonies wh[ich] I am old fashioned enough to believe w[oul]d be a national misfortune, & what is more a Misfortune to the civilized world, but to avert this I am sure it is necessary to adopt the policy of cautiously proceeding to throw more of the Military expenditure upon the Colonies. . . . In Canada I do not think we ought to do this yet, but the time for doing so cannot be long delayed; what I wish is, to wait till the present period of commercial depression has passed by as I have no doubt it will do before long, provided tranquillity & Confidence can be maintained. . . . (Earl Grey to Lord Elgin, Governor-General of Canada, 22 August 1849, Public Archives of Canada, as quoted in A. G. Doughty, ed., *The Elgin-Grey Papers 1846-1852*, Ottawa 1937, I, 448)

4. British Emigration and Colonial Settlement

At a time when the British Isles were suffering from severe economic distress and social dislocation, most Englishmen believed that domestic difficulties could be alleviated by means of emigration. Colonies provided convenient outlets for Britain's 'surplus' population, and of the various parts of the empire open to settlers, none appeared more attractive than the provinces of British North America. Contemporaries were faced with the problem, however, of deciding how far the imperial government should actively promote emigration and finance it at the expense of the British taxpayer. The question was frequently discussed in parliament in the 1820's, largely as a result of the untiring efforts of Wilmot Horton, who proposed that English parishes should subsidize the emigration of paupers from local rates levied for the relief of the poor. During debates on emigration in 1827 and 1828, speakers included Robert Torrens, a radical economist interested in colonial matters, and Henry Bright, a Tory politician.

. . . Colonel *Torrens* said, that. . . . He would add one word about the expense of carrying this projected emigration into effect. Great stress had been laid upon this; and some hon. gentlemen appeared to think, that the greatness of the expense would be fatal to the project. He, however, was of opinion, that the expense of sending out a million of people to Canada would be well repaid. They would occupy twenty millions of acres of the best land which government could give them, and if capital were supplied them, these acres would in a few years be worth a pound an acre; and could they not then afford to pay a shilling a year rent? Any body accustomed to consider the value of land, and the growth of rent, would entertain no doubt that to Canada this calculation, at the lowest, would apply. And, as to that noble country, people at home really looked at the question in a very narrow point of view. They looked at Canada simply as she now was, not with any regard to what she might be—to what she must hereafter attain to—in the occupation of a large British population of settlers, going out there with sufficient, though probably frugal, means. . . . Markets for various commodities would be constantly springing up in Canada, and she would, at no distant period, become as flourishing, in proportion to her resources, as the United States. . . .

Mr. *Bright* considered that. . . . The government ought not to shrink from the question of emigration, from any fear of expense. He thought Canada one of the bulwarks of the empire, and it was of the greatest possible moment that she should be adequately colonized and supported, if we meant to protect ourselves in our American possessions, or wished to defend them from encroachment. A large annual sum of money from the public purse, for the advancement and encouragement of this beautiful colony, would be always well expended. . . .

Mr. *Hume* contended, that to employ £20,000,000 in carrying to a foreign country one out of every eighteen members of our population, was a wasteful employment of the public capital, inasmuch as the void occasioned by such a measure would be made up in three years. . . . He likewise argued . . . that at the end of seven years from their first settlement, the emigrants would not be able to repay the government, or their parishes, the expenses of their emigration. The practical result of this project might be, to send away beggars from England, to make beggars of those who remained behind; for what other result could follow from sending £20,000,000 out of the country, which, if left in, would be expended in some way or other among the working classes? Employment must always be in proportion to capital, and when so much floating capital was withdrawn from circulation, a proportionate quantity of employment must be withdrawn from the labouring part of the community. . . . (*Hansard*, New Series, XVI, 15 February 1827, 492, 494-6, 509-10)

. . . Mr. *Wilmot Horton* [said]. . . . The chief objection was, that any plan of emigration would be expensive, and that the finances of the country were not in a condition to bear the advances necessary for that purpose. He denied it would cost any thing; for he considered it would cost nothing, if it involved the repayment of the advance. . . . He undertook to prove, that the maintenance of the labourers and their families, whose labour was not in demand in this country, was a direct tax on the community at large. He estimated that the men, women, and children, taken one with another, were not to be fed, clothed, and lodged, under £3 per head per annum. One hundred thousand of these persons could be removed, it had been calculated, at an expense of £60,000 a-year, laying aside any prospect of re-payment. At present these one hundred thousand persons, at £3 per head, cost the country £300,000 a-year. If for £60,000 they could be removed to the colonies, there would clearly be a saving of £240,000 annually out of the general revenue of the country . . . it would be far more profitable to send out emigrants to cultivate fertile lands in the colonies, than to employ them in bringing into cultivation poor soils in England . . . by mortgaging the poor-rates for a short time, they would be enabled to get rid of the maintenance of the paupers, which was perpetually entailed on them. He wished to observe, that it was not intended by this bill that it should be compulsory on parishes; on the contrary, he wished it merely to be a permissive measure. . . . (*Hansard*, New Series, XVIII, 17 April 1828, 1549-51)

The whole question of subsidized emigration was modified after 1830, when Edward Gibbon Wakefield propounded the theory of systematic colonization, under which British emigration would be financed by revenue from the sale of crown lands in the colonies. This practice was adopted by the Colonial Office in the case of the Australian colonies in 1831-2, but it was decided that the shorter and cheaper journey to North America should not be subsidized by public funds, and it never became so. Particularly revealing of contemporary attitudes was the view frequently propounded by Earl Grey, who had been responsible for the reforms of 1831, that financial intervention by the state might check the existing flow of voluntary emigration to North America, seriously undermine the initiative and self-reliance of individuals, and involve the government in a host of complicated and expensive administrative arrangements.

. . . in what I have now said I have proceeded on the assumption that the Emigration of the present year will be of the same character as that of former years; that is, that it will consist of persons proceeding to America without any direct assistance from H M Govt, but provided with the means of emigrating either from their own resources, or by the contributions of their friends, of their Landlords, or in some few instances of Parishes, or [Poor Law] Unions. It is not proposed by Her Majesty's Govt to attempt to give encreased activity to the flow of Emigration to North America by undertaking to provide for Emigrants the means of conveyance, either gratuitously, or at a lower cost than that at which they can obtain it for themselves. . . . It is obvious that if free passages to Canada were offered to Emigrants it would be not only difficult but impossible to confine the boon to those who would otherwise be unable to obtain from other sources the means of Emigration. . . . If passages were provided at the public expense for all who desired to emigrate . . . sacrifices now made by so many persons for the purpose of doing so would cease, and a very large proportion of those who now by some means, or other find their own way across the Atlantic would have to be conveyed at the Public expense. Even those who now proceed directly to the United States would seek the same ultimate destination by the route of Canada in order to avail themselves of the gratuitous passage provided for Emigrants to the British Colonies. . . . At present the emigration is conducted at a very cheap rate. The desire to reach America being exceedingly strong many of the Emigrants are content, in order to do so, to submit to very great hardships during the voyage. . . . If, however, this service were undertaken by the Executive Government the sort of accommodation which is now submitted to without a murmur would not be endured, and a very superior and, therefore, a much more costly conveyance would have to be provided. . . . Nor is this all. It is obvious that H M's Govt could not convey Emigrants to North America without becoming responsible for their not being left destitute when they arrived there. Under the existing system of spontaneous Emigration, Emigrants are aware that on their arrival in Canada they have only themselves to trust to, and that except relief in the Hospital when sick and conveyance from the Port of debarkation to places where their labour may be in demand they have no assistance to look for from the Government. Hence they are led to make every possible exertion to maintain themselves and the result is that a very large number of Emigrants annually find the means of doing so. But for this purpose very strenuous efforts on their part are necessary, nor is it reasonable to suppose that such efforts would be made by them if they felt that the Govt by carrying them to the Colony had incurred a virtual responsibility for their support. . . . This would be the more probable, as providing for Emigrants free passages to Canada would it is to be feared make a great change in the character of the Emigrants. At present it is in general (with the exception of those sent out by parishes and Unions) the strong and the enterprising that emigrate, since these alone will make the efforts necessary for the purpose. But if the means of emigrating were supplied by the public a very different class of Emigrants would make its appearance, the most infirm, or the least industrious are those whom their neighbours at home would be the most anxious to put forward to emigrate; and of course such Emigrants would be far more likely than those who now go to Canada to become dependent upon Charity, and as the burthen could not possibly be thrown upon the Provincial Revenue it must fall upon the British Treasury. Looking at all these charges, and to that of the large establishment which would be necessary to carry on so vast a system of Emigration . . . the probability is that a charge of Two Millions, or more might be thrown upon the Treasury, and what is worse the system of voluntary Emigration which is now working so satisfactorily, and upon so large a scale, would be entirely deranged and might not again, without great difficulty, be restored. . . . (Earl Grey to Lord Elgin, 29 January 1847, Public Record Office, C.O. 43/148, pp.154-65)

Inextricably related to the problems of emigration was the question of settling emigrants in the colonies. Here there emerged a basic difference of opinion: Wilmot Horton and others argued that emigrant labourers should be established as small landed proprietors; Gibbon Wakefield and his supporters maintained that colonial economic and social development demanded that emigrants without substantial capital should be compelled to work as labourers for some time after their arrival in the colonies and be prevented from becoming landowners by the sale of public lands at a sufficiently restrictive price. Horton expressed his view in a parliamentary debate in 1827.

. . . A very mistaken notion was entertained by many persons as to the mode in which emigration should be carried into effect. Those persons maintained that emigration should be conducted on the principle of supplying labourers only to the colonies—that the expense should be limited to the carrying of the emigrants out, and landing them on the shores to be disposed of as chance or circumstances might direct. The principle on which the emigrations of 1823 and 1825 [to Upper Canada] had been conducted was quite different. In both those instances it had been considered wise and necessary to plant the emigrants, and to supply them with capital, not in money, but in kind, to enable them to support themselves, and to accumulate property. In short, to place them in a condition to want labourers for themselves, rather than to become labourers to others. If labourers were wanted, nothing, certainly, could be better than to introduce them up to a certain point; but absorption must soon take place, the market would soon be abundantly supplied with labourers; but no limit could be assigned to the improvement which would result from colonizing upon the principle which had been acted on in 1823 and 1825, unless, indeed, the fertility of the land should become exhausted. That was the distinction which he drew between emigration where the individuals were fixed to the soil, and that desultory kind of emigration which consisted in merely conveying them to a certain place, and then leaving them to make their way as they could. He would appeal to any man whether the advantages of continuing the plan hitherto pursued were not almost too obvious to require argument. The settler would be firmly fixed in the soil, instead of taking his chance of obtaining subsistence. . . . (*Hansard*, New Series, XVI, 15 February 1827, 480-1)

The Wakefieldians, however, wanted to restrict access to landownership, and so preserve a pool of labour for capitalists, because they considered this the only effective method of fostering colonial economic development and the emergence of civilized communities in new countries. The apparent economic stagnation and desolation of life in British North America could be cured only if the government, through the regulations it adopted for the alienation of crown lands, exercised a stricter control over the progress of colonial settlement, the pattern of land utilization, the structure of landownership, and the rate of economic growth. But the success of the Wakefieldians' campaign greatly depended on winning the support of officials at the Colonial Office and persuading them to adopt the principles of systematic colonization as the basis of imperial land administration throughout the empire. The Whig ministers, Lord Goderich and Lord Howick, were initially sympathetic towards Wakefield's ideas. In a series of reforms in 1831, known as the Ripon Land Regulations after Goderich's later title, the sale of crown lands in the colonies by public auction at a relatively restrictive price was adopted as the basis of imperial practice.

Instructions were accordingly sent to the governors in British North America. In a despatch to Lieutenant-Governor Colborne in Upper Canada the new policy was explained in terms very similar to those employed by the Wakefieldians.

. . . It has been urged that to compel the bona fide Settler to pay for his Land anything beyond the necessary expence of surveying it and marking out the limits is to deprive him of a portion of his Capital, which, if allowed to retain it, he might employ to great advantage. Plausible as this objection is, experience has demonstrated that by yielding to it and by making free Grants much more inconvenience is incurred than can arise from this alleged defect in the system of Sale. If no consideration is to be given in return for Land all persons will be desirous to obtain it, and that too in quantities not limited by their ability to turn it to advantage. Either therefore land must be lavished in a manner which will quickly leave none unappropriated and open for the occupation of those who can really make use of it, or a power must be entrusted to the Executive Government of deciding what claims are to be admitted and what rejected. To such a power being placed in any hands there are the strongest objections, it gives a species of patronage to its possessors almost without responsibility since its due exercise is with difficulty to be distinguished from its abuse, and . . . exposes to suspicion even the most perfect impartiality and fairness. . . . It is likewise found, practically, that under the system I am now considering no degree of caution is sufficient to prevent large tracts of Land from getting into the possession of persons whose object it is not to improve it, but at a future day to dispose of it, when it shall have acquired an encreased value from the Settlement and improvement of the vicinity; the effect of this being to enable the idle or fraudulent Proprietor not only to put his more industrious Neighbours to great inconvenience, but also to derive a profit from their exertions to which he has in justice not the slightest claim. . . .

The example of the United States has shewn that without any of the complicated Regulations, by which it has been attempted to guard against the misapplication of Land acquired gratuitously, without those conditions and restraints which have been equally inoperative in the prevention of fraud and inconvenient to the bona fide Settler, we may safely trust to the interest of the purchasers as a sufficient security that the land which has been paid for will be turned to good account.

It has been said that by a strict adherence to this system, by refusing land to the poor Man whose labor is his only wealth, a most useful Class of Settlers will be discouraged. I see no ground for such an apprehension; whatever promotes the prosperity of the Colony will naturally attract Settlers both of the labouring and of all other Classes; nor do I see any reason to suppose that the former will consider it any hardship to be required to pay for the land which they require, whilst its price is moderate, and while wages are so high as to enable them, if industrious, to earn in no long period the means of purchasing it. Has it on the other hand been sufficiently considered by those who make this objection, whether it would conduce to the real prosperity of the Province to encourage every man who can labor to do so only on his own account, to obtain and cultivate his allotment of land without giving or receiving assistance from others? Without some division of labor, without a class of persons willing to work for wages, how can Society be prevented from falling into a state of almost primitive rudeness and how are the comforts and refinements of civilized life to be preserved? Declining, however, to proceed in the discussion of this question any further, I must observe that the price paid by the Settler for his land is not in fact lost to him, it is applied in diminishing the burthens of taxation by defraying part of the necessary expences of the Government, and it will also, it is to be hoped, afford the means of opening Roads, of erecting Schools and Churches and of making other local improvements. . . . (Lord Goderich to Sir John Colborne, 21 November 1831, No. 55, Public Record Office, C.O.43/43, pp. 194-6, 199-201)

Whatever Wakefieldian sympathies it may have had in 1831, the Colonial Office never effectively introduced a restrictive land system into British North America. The amount of land already alienated and the continuing effects of past abuses rendered the new sales regulations largely inoperative. Nevertheless, it was widely argued that if the Canadian colonies were to remain suitable outlets for English emigration, and if an extensive programme of systematic colonization was going to be adopted, the British government had to maintain some authority over the distribution of colonial lands. Although control over this vital area of administration had soon to be surrendered to the colonists, many Englishmen felt that these lands belonged to the empire at large and should be managed for imperial rather than for purely local purposes.

. . . the interest of the parent state in the waste lands of her colonies does not cease with their alienation—does not cease until those waste lands are covered with people. Until that be done, the parent state has a claim on those lands; they do not belong exclusively or chiefly to the colonists. . . .

. . . A highly-civilized and densely-peopled state possesses extensive waste lands in the colonies. Those lands derive their value in part from their natural qualities and geographical features, but still more from the acquired resources of the parent country. . . . In a state possessing those waste lands, all citizens have equal rights— all have a share in the collective right to those waste lands; and if a few hundreds or even thousands by settlement acquire a further right of occupancy in certain parts of those lands, that right cannot extend to deprive the whole community at home of its interest in the whole. . . .

. . . The wants of a colonial community are correlative with those of the parent state: she wants space of land; they, labour and capital; and the same process which appropriates to the use of the parent state the waste lands of the colony, conveys to them the labour and capital which they lack. . . . The true connexion between a colony and a parent state consists in this efflux, until the distribution of people and capital upon land has in an approximate degree been equalized. . . . (*Spectator*, 18 September 1847)

II   THE GOVERNMENT OF COLONIES

1. Imperial Administration

Discussion of Britain's government of the empire involved not only imperial policies but also the institutions at home and overseas which administered those policies. The two main agencies in London responsible for colonial affairs were parliament and the Colonial Office. While parliament's legislative authority could be employed as an instrument of British supremacy throughout the empire, many Englishmen maintained that imperial measures were seldom discussed in an enlightened and constructive manner. The evils of this situation were condemned in 1849 by the *Colonial Magazine*, a non-party journal devoted to news and comment about the empire.

. . . colonial questions differ altogether in kind from questions of domestic interest. In the latter case it may be sufficient to allow opinion to come to maturity, until "questions solve themselves"; but in the former there is an obviously different duty to be discharged. Public opinion, which in fact only means the decision of the average of society upon matters affecting their own interest, and of which they may be presumed to have an average practical experience, is not likely to arrive at any useful determination on a subject of remote interest and only contingent advantage. A policy, therefore, will not form itself out of hap-hazard legislation for the colonies, because such legislation does not and can not represent really the progressive education of the public mind and the development of general principles. Temporary expedients and experimental Acts of Parliament can be made use of in the Home Government, because they will be always rectified as occasion may require by the practical good sense of the people; they are an addition to the sum of political knowledge. But in legislation for the colonies, a similar process is wholly ineffectual; the failure of the experiment is not witnessed by those who make it, and is, therefore, not corrected; it increases the amount of ignorance and uncertainty. The interference of the Imperial Legislature is, therefore, for the most part, ineffectual or mischievous; besides which, there always exists the possibility of a colonial question becoming the battle-field of party. Thus, either from ignorance in the one case, or indifference in the other, the colony and its real interests may be sacrificed. . . . It has often been said that the Colonial Office is subject to sinister influences, but Parliament is infinitely more so, on a matter in which constituencies take no interest. Thus a great commotion may be made in the House by the personal influence exercised by the projectors of a land or colonising company: sometimes, again, a clique of merchants residing in this, their native city, may contrive to dictate a policy; at other times, the power of Exeter Hall [missionary interests] may be brought to bear with the most pernicious results to the unfortunate colonist. Now, each and all of these forces tend at different times to thwart the good intentions and to bias the judgment of the most

upright and intelligent politicians, and much as it may be regret-
ted, Parliament is far more liable to be influenced by them than
any minister, however ignorant and incompetent he may be. The
House of Commons is more irresponsible than the Colonial Office,
and is unable to apply to colonial affairs a tenth part of the experience possessed by the subordinates of that long-suffering and much-
abused department. . . . ("Imperial and Colonial Policy", *Colonial
Magazine*, XVII, 1849, 63-64)

It was widely held that the conduct of ministers and permanent
officials at the Colonial Office was not subject to wholesome scrutiny
and supervision. Englishmen of all shades of political opinion argued
from time to time that the permanent staff of the colonial department
exercised an arbitrary and irresponsible authority over the empire. In
1838, Sir William Molesworth, a leading radical politician, criticized
the shortcomings of this imperial bureaucracy.

. . . He had enumerated a series of grievous wrongs inflicted on
the Canadian people by the tools of the Colonial Office, and for
which the Ministers who had presided over that department of the
State ought to be held strictly responsible. But it should be remarked
that of all the high functionaries the Colonial Secretary was the one
least exposed to effective responsibility, because the people of a
mother country are necessarily uninterested and unacquainted with
the affairs of their remote dependencies. Therefore it was only on
extraordinary occasions that the public attention could be directed
from matters of nearer interest to colonial concerns: it was rarely
that the Colonial Office could be made to feel the weight of public
opinion, and to fear censure and exposure. Where, however, responsibility was wanting, the experience of all ages had proved, that
abuses would exist, and continue to exist, unredressed, until at last
they reached that amount which induced them [the colonists] no
longer to trust to prayer and humble petition, but raise the cry of
war, and have recourse to arms. Such had been the case of Canada.
In that province for the last thirty years acknowledged abuses had
existed; acknowledged by Committees, and by Members of every
party in the House of Commons. Great changes had taken place in
the Government of this country, yet no changes had taken place in
the administration of colonial affairs. The same odious system of
colonial misgovernment which was pursued by the Tories had been

acted upon by the Whigs. The causes for the continuance of the same colonial system under Ministers of the most adverse principles were easily to be explained. The Colonial Secretary seldom remained long enough in his office to become acquainted with the concerns of the numerous colonies which he governed. In the last ten years there had been no less than eight different Colonial Secretaries. They had seldom, therefore, the time, and still more seldom the inclination, to make themselves acquainted with the complicated details of their office; their ignorance rendered them mere tools in the hands of the permanent Under-Secretaries and other clerks. It was in the dark recesses of the Colonial Office—in those dens of peculation and plunder—it was there that the real and irresponsible rulers of the millions of inhabitants of our colonies were to be found. Men utterly unknown to fame, but for whom, he trusted, some time or other, a day of reckoning would come, when they would be dragged before the public, and punished for their evil deeds. These were the men who, shielded by irresponsibility, and hidden from the public gaze, continued the same system of misgovernment under every party which alternately presided over the destinies of the empire. By that misgovernment they drove the colonies to desperation—they connived at every description of abuse, because they profited by abuse —they defended every species of corruption, because they gained by corruption. These men he now denounced as the originators and perpetrators of those grievances in Canada, the evil effects of which this country had already begun to experience. He trusted the experience thus gained would convince the people of the necessity of a sweeping reform in the Colonial Office. . . . (*Hansard*, 3rd Series, XL, 23 January 1838, 384-6)

The bureaucracy of the Colonial Office was especially criticized for encouraging imperial patronage and the appointment of ill-qualified and unsuitable governors. As a writer on colonial affairs argued in 1848, defects in the existing system of imperial administration were compounded by the selection of unqualified personnel to operate it.

. . . But it is not with the legislation of Parliament, or the inefficiency of the Colonial Office, that the misrule and evils of our present Colonial system solely rests; the executive officers largely aid in promoting them, and will continue to do so as long as matters are managed as at present. The Colonies are made use of as a means of providing for the younger sons and relatives of the aristocracy, and retired officers in the army and navy. Scarce one of our Colonies can be pointed out which is not governed by old officers, who, from their profession, may well be supposed to understand little of commerce, by which these possessions exist. A more unsuitable person than a rigid old *martinet,* accustomed to all the formalities and strict discipline of military life, can scarce be pointed out for the government of an enterprising, pushing, industrious body of men, who seek, by Colonisation, to benefit themselves, and extend the dominion of their native land. The minor situations are filled up, either with other retired officers, or young men whose only recommendation is their connection with some aristocratic family, or the influence of their friends; and these men generally turn out gross incapables, or, by their assumption and prejudices, disgust and annoy the inhabitants. This, certainly, is not as it should be. . . .

. . . Diplomacy is not entrusted to mere tyros; its followers must serve a long apprenticeship, and pass through many graduations of rank, before they are qualified to be entrusted with any mission of importance. But, alas for the Colonies! any needy scion of a noble race, or eminent old officer whose military services entitle him to reward, is regarded as quite capable of governing a valuable Colony, where thousands of British subjects are located, and millions of British property sunk. All this is wrong, radically, truly bad, and impolitic, and has led to the present deplorable misgovernment and disaffected state of our Colonial Empire. . . . (J. C. Byrne, "The British Colonies, Colonial Office Policy, and Colonial Agents", *Simmond's Colonial Magazine,* XIII, January-April 1848, 135)

2. Problems of the Canadian Constitution, 1828-37

The inherent defects of imperial bureaucracy and centralization were reinforced by the unsatisfactory form of local government existing in many overseas possessions. In British North America and many other settlement colonies with representative institutions, elected assemblies often clashed with nominated councils until acceptance of the principle of responsible government during the 1840's offered an effective means of reconciling their differences. The problems of the Canadian constitution again came into prominence and produced political repercussions in Britain as a result of the increasingly authoritarian administration of the Earl of Dalhousie in Lower Canada and the successful parliamentary demands in 1828 for a select committee of the House of

Commons to inquire into the civil government of Canada. In May of that year a major debate covered many aspects of the Canadian question and examined the nature of British interests in North America. William Huskisson, the liberal-Tory colonial secretary, introduced the debate, and other speakers included Henry Labouchere, Sir James Mackintosh, a radical member and spokesman for the Canadian reformers, Wilmot Horton, Edward Stanley, later a Tory colonial secretary, and Joseph Hume.

Mr. Secretary *Huskisson* said. . . . In contemplating the nature of the constitution provided for the Canadas, we must always bear in mind the great and leading principle on which this country has ever acted, in regard to her political relations, both foreign and domestic—I mean the maintenance of national honour and good faith. In this case it is necessary for us to maintain the good faith of the engagements entered into by this country with the French settlers, who constituted the original population of these colonies; at the same time that we endeavoured, as far as was consistent with these engagements, to introduce among them the benefits to be derived from a system of British law, jurisprudence, and civil administration; a system which has already advanced the prosperity of this country, and her other dependencies to so unparalleled an extent. Nor can there be any difficulty in our examining fully and fairly into all the merits and demerits of the system of government at present prevailing in these valuable colonies, or in our applying an adequate remedy to the evils that may be found to exist; for by the constitution given to the Canadas by parliament in 1791, the legislature of England reserved to itself the liberty to alter, vary, and amend, the government of those colonies as it might think proper. I state this, not upon any abstract or general reasoning that might be applied to the subject, because there must be a paramount power in parliament to redress wrongs in any dependencies of the empire, and to establish any system necessary for the welfare of the subject. . . . I am the rather disposed to rejoice at this circumstance, because, standing aloof, as we do, from the party feelings and local jealousies of the Canadians, our decision will be the more respected; first, as coming from a high and competent authority; and next, on account of our manifest impartiality. On both these grounds I am satisfied that the final determination of parliament, in regard to the civil government of the Canadas, will be cheerfully received, and readily acquiesced in. . . .

... I beg only to add a word or two, respecting a point which has been insinuated in this House, and discussed in other places. I allude to what has been said respecting the policy of giving up the colony altogether. Those who think it would be politic to do so, may say that we ought to spare ourselves the trouble of improving the state of the provinces, by taking the wiser course of relinquishing them altogether. Let those who argue thus, consider that the inhabitants are our fellow subjects—and willing to fulfil all the obligations that their sworn allegiance to the Crown requires. I say that, whilst that is the case, they are entitled to claim from us that protection which their fidelity and good conduct have rendered them so worthy of. On the present occasion, I will not dilate on the importance of the connexion, in a naval, political and commercial, point of view, but I must remind the House, that the political honour, the good faith of this country, are pledged to the protection and support of the Canadian provinces, and warn them of the moral effect which will be produced throughout Europe and the world, by our voluntary relinquishment, if it may not rather be called abandonment, of our dominion over that quarter of the globe. . . . Whether Canada is to remain for ever dependent on England, or is to become an independent State—not, I trust, by hostile separation, but by amicable arrangement—it is still the duty and interest of this country to imbue it with English feeling, and benefit it with English laws and institutions. . . .

Mr. *Labouchere* said, that he fully admitted that the parliament of Great Britain, in what Mr. Burke had termed its imperial capacity, possessed the power of interference and control over all the subordinate legislatures of our colonies, but he thought that this power should be used with extreme caution, and only on a clear case being made out of the imperative necessity for such interference. . . . He hoped that he should have the satisfaction of hearing that right hon. gentleman [Huskisson] declare more distinctly that he had no intention of taking these colonies by surprise, or to make any material alteration in their laws and constitutional rights, without giving them an opportunity of expressing their opinions upon such alteration . . . that nothing would be done until they knew what the colonies themselves wished. If we could not keep the Canadas with the good-will of the inhabitants, we could not keep them at all. He hoped that this all-important truth would never be lost sight of in any measure to be proposed. . . .

Sir *James Mackintosh* said. . . . My maxims of colonial policy are few and simple. A full and efficient protection from all foreign influence; full permission to conduct the whole of their own internal affairs; compelling them to pay all the reasonable expenses of their own government, and giving them, at the same time, a perfect control over the expenditure of the money; and imposing no restrictions of any kind upon the industry or traffic of the people. These are the only conditions which I would impose in the bond of alliance with the metropolitan government, and the only terms upon which I wish that all of them should be governed. These, too, are the only means by which the hitherto almost incurable evil of all distant governments can be either mitigated or removed. . . .

. . . The right hon. gentleman had addressed himself to the feelings of the House, not with a view to excite our sympathy for the sufferings of the petitioners, but to interest us in behalf of the English inhabitants of Canada; and he has made, in several parts of his speech, allusions to the English settlers in that country, as if they were oppressed by the [French] natives. But I ask, what law has been passed by the Assembly of Lower Canada that is unequal or unjust towards the English settlers? What law applies distinctly to them? As a remedy, is it proposed to change the representation? . . . but would it not be the height of injustice to give them [the English inhabitants] that influence, which the Canadians, from their number and property, ought to possess? Sir, when I hear of an inquiry on account of measures necessary to protect the English settlers, I greatly lament that any such language should be used; and I should regard it as a very bad symptom if the House were disposed to treat as a favoured race, as a ruling caste, any body of men, and to look on them as placed in one of our colonies to watch over the rest of the inhabitants. Shall we have an English colony in Canada separate from the rest of the inhabitants? Shall . . . we deal out to them six hundred years of misery, as we had dealt out to Ireland, from having in that country an English colony with English sympathies and English interests? Let us not, in God's name, introduce such curses into another region. Let the policy of this country be, to give to all classes equal law and equal justice; and let it not be supposed that the native Canadians are less entitled to be considered subjects of the king, or less entitled to the protection of the law, than the English inhabitants. . . .

Mr. *Wilmot Horton* said, the . . . right hon. gentleman had argued, that because the colony was French—because it had fallen into our hands by conquest—it ought to remain French to the end of time. Now, he thought it became that House to declare, what plan of colonial policy it was their intention to pursue. . . . The argument was, that the colony was French, the laws were French. He admitted this; and also that a settler, even if an Englishman, was bound by those laws. But this did not prevent parliament from interfering to modify those laws; else what became of the right hon. member's reasoning respecting the Dutch laws of the Cape of Good Hope, or the Spanish laws of Trinidad, which he declared it scandalous for an Englishman to be subjected to, as being contrary to all his feelings and prejudices. For himself, he would never flinch from the proposition that all our colonies should be Anglicised rather than preserved in their original form. The quotation from Mr. Pitt [at the time of passing the constitutional act in 1791] convinced him, that the idea of that great man was, that the French Canadians would, in the course of time, become imbued with English feelings and sentiments, and that their laws would be changed progressively, until they became assimilated to those of England. But it had been decidedly the contrary. . . .

Mr. *Stanley* said, that. . . . The division of the two Canadas he held to be a great mistake. The attempt to form a permanent separation between the Upper and Lower Canadas was a most mischievous measure. While it professed to endeavour to keep out of Lower Canada British capital and industry, it allowed British subjects to settle in the unclaimed and uninclosed lands in the several townships, and thus it opened the way for the introduction of British capital and industry. While in fact, then, it gave an apparent temporary advantage to one class, it afforded a tacit encouragement to the introduction of another class of persons, whose habits of industry and enterprise were calculated to render them superior, and towards whom, as being their own countrymen, the members of the government might exhibit feelings of partiality. The evils which might naturally be expected from such a system had been the result; and the consequence was, that the governor had been compelled to govern that province by a minority, and against the feelings of the great majority of the population. When the government turned its attention to the settlement of the representation in Canada, a difficulty presented itself to the formation of a House of Lords, as there existed no hereditary aristocracy there, and the existence of the

French feudal law opposed an effectual bar to the establishment of any aristocracy. To remedy this evil the Legislative Council was instituted, to supply the place of a House of Lords. How ill that Council had discharged that office, they might judge from the papers before them. The members of that Council upon every occasion had enrolled themselves on the side of the government, and against the people; they . . . were the means of keeping up a continual system of jarring and contention between the government and the people. This Council was the root of all the evils which had taken place in the administration there during the last ten or fifteen years. . . . It was important, that his majesty's Canadian subjects should not have occasion to look across the narrow boundary that separated them from the United States, and see any thing there to envy. He trusted that, in revising the constitution . . . parliament would bear in mind the principles of a liberal policy, and be checked by none of those considerations, which at home perhaps it was necessary to observe, with respect to previous interests and existing prejudices. There they might begin *de novo*; there they might follow the most unfettered liberality, the soundest and most prudent policy they could adopt; there they might enter into a noble rivalry with the United States. They might thus preserve their friendly relations with Canada, both as to the parent State while she remained a colony, and when in the course of ages she became independent as an ally. . . .

Mr. *Hume* [said]. . . They had established independent legislatures in Canada,—they had given to them all the advantages of a British government, and assimilated them to a British House of Commons. Were these houses of assembly to have the free conduct of their affairs, or were they to be subjected to the control of the executive government? Were these legislative bodies to be mere ciphers? What was their use, if all the legislative power was to be lodged in the hands of the executive? He was firmly convinced that his majesty's government had been the cause of all the fermentation and irritation in the Canadas. . . . The colonial policy of the government for some time had been any thing but conciliatory. With the exception of Nova Scotia, was there a single colony from which they had not loud and frequent complaints? If a system of conciliation had been pursued towards the Canadas, the condition of that colony would have been far different from that which it now presented. It was the duty as well as the interest of the government to conciliate the population of Canada, instead of driving them to despair by acts of severity and oppression. . . . (*Hansard*, New Series, XIX, 2 May 1828, 300-2, 314-20, 328-40)

After 1830 successive ministries attempted to grapple with the developing crisis in Lower Canada. Despite their lack of success, British interests in North America and the principles of imperial policy did become more clearly delineated, though the means of attaining them remained illusive. These objectives were enunciated in a minute drawn up in 1836 for the Melbourne cabinet by James Stephen, the permanent under-secretary at the Colonial Office, and in a despatch of 1835 from Lord Aberdeen, the colonial secretary, to Lord Amherst, whom the short-lived Tory ministry at one time intended to send to administer Lower Canada.

The ultimate objects of the Policy of the British Government in relation to the North American Provinces, are few and simple. Every end which is really desirable would be fully accomplished, if adequate security could be taken for maintaining the connexion between the two Countries as Members of the same Monarchy—if the outlet for poor emigrants could be kept open—and if those Commercial interests which may be supposed to depend upon the Colonial character of the Canadas, of New Brunswick, and of Nova Scotia, could be protected.

In pursuing these objects, no measure could be prudently taken with a view to its effect upon a single Province only. The interests of the whole are so complicated with each other, that for any such purpose they must be regarded as one great Community.

No settlement of the existing controversies is fit to be adopted which would provide nothing better than a momentary respite from existing embarrassments. A short truce which had no tendency to bring about an abiding pacification, would rather exasperate than cure the disorder.

The population of British North America is not less than 1,200,000 souls. They are already assuming a distinct National character; and the day cannot be very remote when an Independence, first real, and then avowed, will take the place of the present subjection of these Provinces to the British Crown. The tendency . . . is one from which it would be equally unwise and useless to avert our thoughts. A forecasting Policy would appear to suggest that provision should be deliberately, though of course unavowedly, made for the peaceful and honourable abdication of a power, which ere long it will be impossible to retain; and for raising up on the North American Continent a counterpoise to the United States.

In a paper which has been drawn up on this occasion, another general principle is stated in the following terms:—"The British Colonies in North America are fast rising into considerable States, and already are far too powerful to be governed upon any principle but that of deference for the wishes and opinions of the great Body of the inhabitants. The authority of the Mother Country rests altogether upon the respect and voluntary obedience of her Colonial subjects."

Finally, the present is an occasion in which inaction is probably the most hazardous policy which could be pursued. To do nothing is indeed easy; but to determine that nothing shall be done, is impossible. In such a current there is no resting on the Oars: If its force can neither be stemmed nor directed, it will infallibly hurry every thing before it. . . . (Confidential Minute by Mr. Stephen on Canadian Affairs, 30 April 1836, Public Record Office C.O.537/137, ff. 29-30)

. . . at this distance from the place it is more important clearly to enounce the general principles by which H.M.'s Government are directed than to prescribe the particular measures which they may desire to adopt or to sanction. Those Principles are few and simple. They consist in maintaining inviolate the spirit of the parliamentary Charter of 1791—in deprecating all unnecessary parliamentary legislation respecting the internal affairs of Lower Canada—in transferring to the Representatives of the People the utmost possible control over the produce of all the duties levied within the Province, & of all branches of the Public Revenue arising there—in discountenancing all favor shewn to any one Class of the Inhabitants to the prejudice of the rest—and in making the prosperity of the Province with the Conciliation of the Inhabitants to each other and to this Kingdom, the only object to be borne in view in the Administration of the Government of that part of H. M.'s Dominions. (Lord Aberdeen to Lord Amherst, 2 April 1835, No. 2, Public Record Office, C.O.43/30)

Under the constitution of 1791, the governments of Upper and Lower Canada consisted of a governor, executive council, legislative

council, and assembly, which were intended to be the colonial counter-
parts of the British institutions of sovereign, cabinet, Lords, and Commons. But while the outward forms of the British constitution might
be transplanted in Canada, complete assimilation was never possible.
Traditional British institutions did not necessarily meet the needs of
pioneering communities or suit the character of the more open "democratic" and ethnically diverse type of society that emerged in the North
American colonies. No hereditary aristocracy existed in Canada to
provide the basis of a provincial House of Lords; whereas the imperial
parliament, still elected on a narrow franchise, represented the pro-
pertied classes, colonial assemblies were more popular in character and
the majority of the people already had the vote. Even without the dis-
tracting influence of American ideas and republican practices from
across the border, the governments of Britain and Canada could never
be identical. Indeed, by the 1830's the divergence between governments
was particularly noticeable; cabinet government and ministerial responsibility became accepted British conventions but were not yet
thought appropriate or practicable in colonial dependencies. The two
major proposals, advanced by the Canadian reformers to resolve the
constitutional deadlock between councils and assemblies that had
emerged by the thirties, involved changing the composition of the
legislative council and rendering the executive council responsible to
the assembly. Until the eve of the rebellions in 1837, alterations in the
membership of the legislative council formed the principal demand of
the reformers in Lower Canada, who believed that effective political
power rested in the legislative body rather than in the executive council.
While the Whigs tried to improve its composition, the British government was not prepared to accept demands for an elective legislative
council, which would become a replica of the assembly, and, in the
case of Lower Canada, would have produced a French majority in
both houses to the detriment of British settlers in the province. The
arguments in favour of this radical step were presented by J. A. Roebuck, who was appointed parliamentary agent for the assembly of
Lower Canada in 1835.

> . . . There was only one way to bind the people of Canada per-
> manently to this country, and that was by redressing their manifold
> grievances. Let the British Parliament do what he demanded—let
> it alter the constitution of the Legislative Council. What harm could
> result from the adoption of his proposition? It had been said, that

that Council was a means of cementing the union between the colony and the mother country; but the truth was, that all its acts were calculated to irritate the feelings of the people of Canada, and tended to separate the two countries. But by rendering the Legislative Council elective, it would be made acceptable to the people, and its conduct would naturally be such as to conciliate their affections. The objection to this course of proceeding was, that it was American—that it was republican. How puerile was that sort of argument! By what magic was an aristocracy to be formed in Canada? An aristocracy could not be created in a day; it was not to be raised like asparagus; it must be the growth of an age. The aristocracy of England was not an aristocracy of yesterday, but had existed ever since England was a nation; and yet the influence of this ancient aristocracy, so far from extending, was daily diminishing; while the feeling of equality gained ground. If such were the case in this country, was it to be expected that an aristocracy could be maintained in a new nation? The existence of two parties in Canada—the French party and the English party—was put forward as a ground for preserving the Legislative Council, because it was said, that body represented the English party—the French being represented in the House of Assembly; and the application of the elective principle to the Legislative Council would be favourable to the French party, and render it too predominant in the Legislature. He begged the House to consider whether this objection to his proposition was well founded. The number of persons speaking the English language in Lower Canada was 134,000 and odd, and the number of persons speaking the French language, 374,932; so that the English party was about one-third of the amount of the French party. The House of Assembly contained eighty-eight members, sixty-four of whom were said to be of French origin, all the rest being of English origin; so that the English party constituted as nearly as possible one-third of the representation. But then it was said that all those English Members did not vote with the Government. That was undoubtedly the case; and the same complaint was made in Upper Canada, where there were no French, which plainly proved that the demands made by the people of Canada did not proceed from narrow party considerations, but were founded on principle and justice. The fact was, that the Legislative Council was merely the representative of a small clique, the official partisans of the Government, by whom every thing was done to irritate the people. . . . It was quite clear, in the natural course of things, that the Canadas and England could not remain joined together, as they now were, but for a very small number of years. The only union that would hereafter exist between these countries, would be that arising out of their commercial intercourse with one another. That connexion might be continued; but if England should attempt to continue the union by the present system of rule, it would only be the means of inducing the Canadians to make a comparison between their condition and that of other and neighbouring nations, and of the great benefits derived under the form of government which prevailed in those countries, the result of which would inevitably be, that the connexion between England and her North American colonies would come to a rapid, and, he was afraid, a violent dissolution. . . . (*Hansard*, 3rd Series, XXXIII, 16 May 1836, 928-30)

The seemingly insurmountable objections to the creation of an elective council were put forward in a confidential minute written for the cabinet in 1834 by Robert Hay, a man of strong Tory opinions, who was permanent under-secretary at the Colonial Office until 1836.

. . . I am fully disposed to admit that all reasonable demands, or reasonable remonstrances of the colonists should be attended to, but where they are of a contrary character, which I am sorry to say is too much the case in Lower Canada, more evil than good must follow from concession . . . the time is now arrived when, if the home government do not adopt some steady course of policy in regard to our North American provinces, a succession of tormenting controversies with each province will arise, and, in the end, the whole of them will slip away from this country's dominion. . . .

Next to finance, in importance, is the question of rendering the legislative council elective, as prayed for by the assembly. I am aware that until this point be given up, there will be no peace in Canada; but, nevertheless, as government must make a stand somewhere, a better ground cannot be taken than this. . . .

The provincial assembly being chosen by the people, I can see no possible advantage which they can derive from, nor claims which they can possess to, a second deliberative body of a similar character; and, however difficult it may be to produce an assembly in any of our provinces which may resemble, in any degree, the British house of peers, surely the establishment of the principle of election for the upper house would be the most certain mode of rendering any approximation to it in future time utterly out of the question. Mr. Stephen seems to doubt whether any such body, as the legislative council of Lower Canada is constituted, would obtain any respect from the people, unless it originated from themselves. I am inclined to think otherwise, and that if distinctions of rank were dispensed by the higher powers in Canada, they would be looked up to;—although, undoubtedly, not in the same degree as where an hereditary aristocracy challenges respect, not only from its own claim, but from the habits of deference which long usage has established. . . . (Hay's Confidential Minute on Lower Canada, 22 September 1834, Public Record Office, C.O.537/137, f.27)

The demand for an executive council responsible to the assembly did not occupy such a prominent place in contemporary discussion until the eve of the Canadian rebellions. Nevertheless, the British government firmly rejected the idea as being inconsistent with the status of a colonial dependency and the preservation of the imperial connection. The arguments against this reform were expounded by Lord John Russell in March 1837.

. . . It is proposed . . . that the executive council should be made to resemble the ministry in this country. I hold this proposition to be entirely incompatible with the relations between the mother country and the colony. The relations between the mother country and the colony require that his Majesty should be represented not by a person removable by the House of Assembly, but by a governor sent out by the King, responsible to the King and responsible to the Parliament of Great Britain. This was the necessary constitution of a colony; and if you have not these relations existing between the mother country and the colony you will soon have an end to the relations altogether. Then, again, if the executive council were made responsible as the ministers of this country, of course the governor must act according to their advice. If the Assembly do not trust those ministers, if they do not think them fit, they must be removed, and others put in their places. The person sent out by the king as governor, and those ministers in whom the assembly confided, might differ in opinion, and there at once would be a collision between the measures of the King and the conduct of the representatives of the colony. But this proposition would tend not merely to produce disputes, not merely to try the King's authority, but it would tend to introduce authorities totally incompatible with the authority which the King seems to have over every colony. . . . That part of the constitution which requires that the Ministers of the Crown shall be responsible to Parliament, and shall be removable if they do not obtain the confidence of Parliament, is a condition which exists in an imperial legislature, and in an imperial legislature only. It is a condition which cannot be carried into effect in a colony—it is a condition which can only exist in one place, namely, the seat of empire. Otherwise we should have separate independent powers existing not only in Great Britain, but in every separate colony. In such a case the Government would be unable to carry its measures or wishes into effect, and each colony would, in effect, be an independent state. . . . (*Hansard*, 3rd Series, XXXVI, 6 March 1837, 1294-5)

3. British Reactions to the Rebellions

The outbreak of the rebellions in Lower and Upper Canada in December 1837 at last gave the British government a free hand to impose its own settlement. These events in Canada naturally led Englishmen to examine such questions as the causes and justification for the revolts, the ministry's responsibility for precipitating the crisis, the likely outcome for Britain's position in North America, and the points of contrast and comparison with the American Revolution. In the parliamentary debates of the time, two contrasting views on events were presented by William Gladstone, then a Tory member, and John Leader, a radical spokesman.

. . . The question was, whether in a country where no practical oppression was proved to exist—where person and property had been secure, and would be so, at this moment, but for the machinations of popular agitators—where the law was duly administered, and where the taxes were mild or none at all—they were, for the sake, and on the ground, of speculative and organic changes, which promised no advantage to the colonies, and which must prove utterly destructive of the analogy and harmony which had existed between the mother country and the Canadians, to be terrified from maintaining that which they believed to be just on the first manifestation

of the spirit of insurrection. . . . There were those, too, in the colonies whose interests they were bound to protect. Let it not be supposed that he meant to contend that this island should have distant portions of the globe for ever dependent upon it; but the time when a separation on the part of Canada might be beneficial had not certainly arrived at the present period, when her population was divided into two parties of different origin, and inflamed by their passions into continual collision with each other. In this state of things, this country was enabled by her power to act as a mediator and umpire, and thus prevented contests which might be found still more fatal. . . . He refrained from going into particulars relative to the insurrection in the United States; but he must say, that the whole resistance of the American people was based on irrefutable facts, and on statements of positive and palpable grievances; and the abstract rights of man, such as they conceived them to be, were appealed to in support of the facts which had been previously stated. Let it, then, be shown that practical grievances existed in the case of the Canadians. . . .
(*Hansard*, 3rd Series, XXXIX, 22 December 1837, 1454-5)

. . . For many years past, the Canadians have complained of numerous grievances, and, having first petitioned in vain, they at last demanded redress. Although every one of their complaints was admitted to be well founded, their prayers were neglected, their demands were treated as unreasonable; they were too weak to command attention, for they were not considered strong enough to enforce redress. For many years they went on petitioning in vain; trusting to the generosity of England, and hoping for relief, till even the hope of justice from England seems to have left them, then, and not till then, having discovered the fruitlessness of supplication, they had recourse to that legal power which their constitution gave them, and they refused to vote any money for a Government which had obstinately refused to accede to their just demands. In doing this, they exercised a known, recognised, legal right, conferred upon them by the constitution which England had given them. You say they used their right improperly and at an improper time, and therefore you coerce them; but you are not to make yourselves judges of the time and manner in which a constitutional assembly is to exercise a legal right. . . . The North American provinces are now strong enough to take care of themselves, and they know it. Is it then prudent to insist on keeping them in political subjection for a short time longer, knowing that they must soon be independent, and that if coerced now they will be hostile to England for many years—and that if an amicable separation be effected now, while it will anticipate the period of their independence but by a few years, it will render them sure friends to England, and convert their country from a burdensome colony into a most profitable free market for our manufactures, and a better and a more inviting field than now for emigration? The question, then, is now no longer one between parties in the colony only—it is no longer a question of right between the popular and the official parties, nor between the majority and the minority—nor, as the Government would have it appear, between the French and English races. It has become a great and urgent question between the Government and the people of England, whether the Government shall or shall not be permitted to plunge the country into a contest, indefensible on any principle of justice, and likely to involve us in a general war. Will the people consent to the pouring forth of blood and treasure to uphold the authority of the Colonial-office, or to gratify the love of dominion, or at best to keep in unwilling subjection an expensive colony? . . . Whatever may be the result of the contest, I rejoice that the Canadians have resisted. Half a million of people so dead to all the feelings of liberty as voluntarily to submit to be slaves, would have been fit instruments to make slaves of the rest. The noble Lord [Russell] remembers similar words; he remembers by whom, and on what occasion they were used more than seventy years ago; he remembers the events of that period; but he seems to have forgotten or disregarded the warning indelibly stamped by them on the tablet of history. In defiance of experience, his Government is pursuing now the very course which then led to disaster and disgrace; and if they obstinately persevere in that course, I trust and verily believe that, even should they escape immediate and well-merited punishment, they will be held up to the scorn and execration of posterity, as the men who, with the example of the struggle for American independence before their eyes, plunged England into a disgraceful and disastrous war, for the purpose of chastising a colony which they had themselves, by their own incompetence, injustice, and misgovernment, forced into open rebellion. (*Hansard*, 3rd Series, XXXIX, 22 December 1837, 1432, 1444-5)

While radical journals such as the *Spectator* emphasized the close parallels between the Canadian rebellions and the American Revolution in the course of attacking the 'Toryfied' policy of the Whig ministry towards Canada, most English commentators questioned the validity of such comparisons and argued that the contest in Lower Canada had its origins in racial antagonisms. An early exponent of this view, which soon became almost unanimously accepted in Britain, was the *Morning Chronicle*.

It cannot be too much impressed on the British public that the contest in Lower Canada is really between the men of French and the men of British descent. The French wish to have Lower Canada exclusively to themselves; and were they to become independent of this country, by not merely beating the QUEEN'S army but the English part of the population, which no sane man can suppose possible, they would strip the English of their grants, and impose such restrictions on the navigation of the St. Lawrence as would of necessity compel the inhabitants of Upper Canada to throw themselves into the arms of the United States. But so sensible are the British inhabitants of Lower and Upper Canada of the injury they would sustain from French ascendancy, that if Government were to remain idle, they would not, and a fierce civil war would be carried on which would probably end in the men of British blood driving their opponents from Canada. . . .

And why do the English Ministers and Parliament refuse to consent to the independence of Great Britain demanded by the French Canadians? Because Lower Canada is not exclusively French, but inhabited also by men of British descent, who have received grants of land in the province from the Crown, and because the river which flows through Lower Canada belongs also to the immense territory of the upper province. . . . To understand why the French Canadians are so anxious to strip their English neighbours of the lands held by them under Crown grants, we must advert to the peculiarity of the Catholic religion which keeps Catholics together. The French Canadians wished to have themselves considered a separate nation, "La nation Canadienne", and to have all the lands considered as belonging to that "nation", to remain waste till required by the "nation" in its progressive and connected development. But the occupation of wastes in the rear of the French "habitans" is in the teeth of this plan, for it compels the French either to remain where they are now settled, or to scatter themselves among the British settlers, an idea quite abhorrent to them. . . .

. . . Such, then, would be the consequences of yielding to the

French Canadians. It is not a question of constitutional liberty; but a question between narrow notions, bigotry, and monopolies of the worst sort, and a liberal system of government—between justice to British citizens and confiscation of their lands and goods. (*Morning Chronicle*, 28 December 1837)

Anti-French sentiment and emphasis on racial antagonisms were reflected both in Lord Durham's analysis of the problems of Lower Canada and in the proposals contained in his *Report*. His recommendation of a union of the Canadas, designed to swamp the French in an English majority, was a product of this widespread British prejudice. Tory newspapers continued to express this attitude most emphatically, and the comments of the *Morning Herald* in April 1840 are typical.

. . . Nothing can be more obvious than that, in legislating for Canada, a mistake of no great apparent magnitude may involve the loss of those invaluable colonies. The great object to be attained is the establishment on the firmest possible footing of British supremacy throughout our North American provinces. It is, of course, most desirable to secure the largest measure of justice to the French Canadians. Their grievances (if such exist) ought at once to be redressed; but they must be made to feel that the ascendancy of British views and opinions is the great end in reference to the Canadas of English policy. As yet it might be unsafe to repose much confidence, during times of danger, in the French Canadians. To the British loyalists alone may we trust; and in a nobler body of colonists did no mother country ever repose confidence. But for the almost superhuman efforts of the loyalist British settlers, the Canadas would, assuredly, during the late convulsions have been transferred to the United States. . . . The Canadas constitute a daily increasing market to the manufactures of England—a market second in steadiness and value only to that which has been created by the home trade. The Canadas maintain the balance of British power; and place the United States in a condition, more or less, of dependence on the political arrangements of England. To abandon the Canadas, would be to invite a general dismemberment of the empire; and if we would avert the necessity for the abandonment of these noble provinces, we must sustain, at all hazards, the ascendancy of the British loyalists, and break down as rapidly as possible, the influence of those associations which, at present, prevent the French Canadians from yielding aught but a grudging obedience to the sway of England. (*Morning Herald*, 14 April 1840)

4. Responsible Government

Lord Durham's recommendation of 'responsible government' in his *Report* of 1839 was not as readily accepted by the British government as his proposal for a union of the Canadas. Durham envisaged that if the colonial executive was made responsible to the popular voice in the assembly and its composition could be changed from time to time to reflect the views of the majority in the legislature, this would offer a means of resolving constitutional conflicts in accordance with prevailing British practice. To facilitate the introduction of this system into a colony, Durham proposed that the fields of administrative responsibility should be divided between the colonial and imperial authorities, so that the former controlled all matters of internal administration, and the latter the few areas of wider imperial concern—specifically, the form of the colonial constitution, the conduct of commercial and foreign relations, and the disposal of public lands.

The precise way in which this system of internal self-government would operate in practice was not clearly spelled out in the Durham *Report*, and considerable controversy at once arose concerning the exact meaning of 'responsible government' and the feasibility of introducing such a system into a colonial dependency where the governor was still considered necessarily accountable for his actions to the authorities in London. Apart from a small group of 'Colonial Reformers', Englishmen generally found it difficult at first to reconcile the proposal with the traditional idea of a colony's dependent status. Indeed, the members of Lord Melbourne's ministry refused to debate the merits of 'responsible government' as a theoretical concept, and insisted that it was a purely practical question on which no further comment was required. The development in Canada of ministries more in harmony with assemblies would be the result of practical politics in the colonies, which only time and experience could satisfactorily determine. This general attitude was reflected in a despatch sent to Governor-General Poulett Thomson in October 1839 by Lord John Russell, the colonial secretary, in which he set out the views of the ministry on the question.

It appears from Sir G. Arthur's despatches that you may encounter much difficulty in subduing the excitement which prevails on the question of what is called "Responsible Government". I have to instruct you, however, to refuse any explanation, which may be construed to imply an acquiescence in the Petitions & Addresses upon this subject. I cannot better commence this despatch than by a reference to the Resolutions of both Houses of Parliament of the 28th April & 9th May in the year 1837 [which denied that a colonial executive could be made responsible to an assembly].

The Assembly of L. Canada having repeatedly pressed this point, H. M. Confidential Advisers at that period thought it necessary not only to explain their views in the communications of the Secretary of State, but expressly called for the opinion of Parliament on the subject. The Crown, & the two Houses of Lords and Commons having thus decisively pronounced a judgment upon the question, you will consider yourself precluded from entertaining any proposition on the subject.

It does not appear indeed that any very definite meaning, is generally agreed upon by those who call themselves the Advocates of this principle, but its very vagueness is a source of delusion, & if at all encouraged would prove the cause of embarrassment & danger.

The Constitution of England, after long struggles & alternate success, has settled into a form of Govt in which the Prerogative of the Crown is undisputed, but is never exercised without advice. Hence the exercise only is questioned, & however the use of the authority may be condemned, the authority itself remains untouched. . . .

But if we seek to apply such a practice to a Colony, we shall at once find ourselves at fault. The power for which a Minister is responsible in England is not his own power, but the power of the Crown, of which he is for the time the organ. It is obvious that the Executive Councillor of a Colony, is in a situation totally different. The Governor under whom he serves, receives his orders from the Crown of England. But can the Colonial Council be the advisers of the Crown of England? Evidently not, for the Crown has other Advisers for the same functions, & with superior authority.

It may happen therefore that the Governor receives at one & the same time instructions from The Queen & advice from his Executive Council totally at variance with each other. If he is to obey his instructions from England, the parallel of constitutional responsibility entirely fails;—if, on the other hand, he is to follow the advice of his

Council, he is no longer a subordinate Officer, but an independent Sovereign.

There are some cases in which the force of these objections is so manifest, that those who at first made no distinction between the Constitution of the United Kingdom & that of the Colonies, admit their strength. I allude to the questions of Foreign War & international relations, whether of Trade or Diplomacy. It is now said that internal Govt is alone intended.

But there are some cases of internal Govt in which the honor of the Crown, or the faith of Parliament, or the safety of the State are so seriously involved, that it would not be possible for Her Majesty to delegate her authority to a Ministry in a Colony.

I will put for illustration some of the cases, which have occurred in that very Province, where the Petition for a responsible Executive first arose—I mean Lower Canada.

During the time when a large majority of the Assembly of L. Canada followed M. Papineau as their Leader, it was obviously the aim of that Gentleman to discourage all who did their duty to The Crown within the Province, & to deter all who should resort to Canada with British habits & feelings from without. I need not say that it would have been impossible for any Minister to support in the Parliament of the United Kingdom the measures which a Ministry headed by M. Papineau would have imposed upon the Governor of L. Canada. British Officers punished for doing their duty —British Emigrants defrauded of their property—British Merchants discouraged in their lawful pursuits—would have loudly appealed to Parliament against the Canadian Ministry & would have demanded protection. . . .

Nor can any one take upon himself to say that such cases will not again occur. The principle once sanctioned, no one can say how soon its application might be dangerous or even dishonorable, while all will agree that to recall the power thus conceded would be impossible.

While I thus see insuperable objections to the adoption of the principle as it has been stated, I see little or none to the practical views of Colonial Govt recommended by Lord Durham, as I understand them. The Queen's Govt have no desire to thwart the Representative Assemblies of B.N. America in their measures of reform & improvement. They have no wish to make those Provinces, the resources for

Patronage at home. They are earnestly intent on giving to the talent & character of leading persons in the Colonies advantages similar to those which talent & character, employed in the public service, obtain in the United Kingdom. Her Majesty has no desire to maintain any system of policy among Her N. A. Subjects, which opinion condemns. . . .

Your Excellency is fully in possession of the principles, which have guided H. M. Advisers on this subject, & you must be aware that there is no surer way of earning the approbation of The Queen than by maintaining the harmony of the Executive with the Legislative Authorities.

While I have thus cautioned you against any declaration from which dangerous consequences might hereafter flow, & instructed you as to the general line of your conduct, it may be said that I have not drawn any specific line, beyond which the power of the Governor on the one hand, & the privileges of the Assembly on the other, ought not to extend. But this must be the case in any mixed Govt. Every political Constitution in which different Bodies share the supreme power is only enabled to exist by the forbearance of those among whom this power is distributed. In this respect the example of England may well be imitated. The Sovereign using the Prerogative of the Crown to the utmost extent, & the House of Commons exerting its power of the Purse to carry all its resolutions into immediate effect, would produce confusion in the Country in less than a twelvemonth. So in a Colony—the Governor thwarting every legimate proposition of the Assembly, & the Assembly continually recurring to its power of refusing Supplies, can but disturb all political relations, embarrass trade, & retard the prosperity of the People. Each must exercise a wise moderation. The Governor must only oppose the wishes of the Assembly, where the Honor of the Crown, or the interests of the Empire are deeply concerned, & the Assembly must be ready to modify some of its measures for the sake of harmony & from a reverent attachment to the authority of Great Britain. (Lord John Russell to C. P. Thomson, 14 October 1839, No. 19, Public Record Office, C.O. 43/35, pp. 94-104)

During the 1840's the implications of responsible government in Canada were gradually acknowledged and accepted amidst the fluctuations of party politics in North America. The method of maintaining harmonious relations with the assembly adopted by Governor-General Thomson, created Lord Sydenham in 1840, was to disrupt political factions and conduct the executive as his own prime minister. English opponents of responsible government found nothing to criticize in this practice, and supporters of the principle expected the governor to play a positive role in colonial politics as leader of the ministry, rather than retire from active politics and become the nominal head of the executive. The first real crisis occurred in 1842 when Sydenham's successor, Sir Charles Bagot, accepted the necessity of admitting into the ministry Louis LaFontaine, the leader of the French Canadians in the assembly, and Robert Baldwin, the leader of a small section of reformers from Canada West. Opinion in England was sharply divided over the wisdom of this move. Supporters of responsible government at once hailed this event as a triumph for their principle, a point of view typically expressed by the *Morning Chronicle.*

. . . the great subject of gratification is the complete triumph of Lord DURHAM'S principle of responsible government, which the recent change recognizes and establishes. The members of the present provincial government are the persons in the province the most obnoxious to the old Tory party. It cannot be supposed that Sir CHARLES BAGOT has selected them from any particular partiality to their views. It is obvious that he has taken them into office solely on account of their possessing the confidence of the majority of the Assembly. The rational system of representative government is, therefore, established in Canada in the most marked manner. The men in whom probably of all in the province the Governor confides the least are taken by him to direct his policy because they are those in whom the people confide the most. A vote of the Legislature in Canada, as in the mother country, now determines who shall wield executive authority. This has been the great subject of conflict hitherto between the Tory and Liberal politicians of the province. It is now decided in favour of the latter. . . .

. . . We do not pretend to predict that the provincial government now constituted will be of long duration, or do much service. We shall be content if its establishment satisfies the majority for a while, and if, when the majority turns against it, it shall make way for those who shall then possess the public confidence. But sure we are that nothing can ensure good government in Canada but a principle which shall thus adapt the constitution of the executive to the variations of public opinion. It was this principle which Lord DURHAM maintained in his Report, and this principle which circumstances compel even his opponents to maintain in practice. (*Morning Chronicle*, 15 October 1842)

The Times, on the other hand, denounced the governor-general for admitting erstwhile rebels into office.

. . . Now, we are great advocates for conciliation, and great opponents of political distinctions founded simply on birth; but it certainly does appear to us that the right, nay, the *only* way to unite to the government and mother country a population of foreign origin, is to select, when it is found necessary officially to employ persons of foreign descent, those amongst them who are most noted, not for preserving or keeping up these distinctions, but for their willingness to wave them; not for their hostility to British connexion, but for their ardent friendship or devoted loyalty. . . . To encourage those among the foreign population who are most disaffected and most anxious for separation is, in fact, no union, it is a widening of the breach; it is no conciliaton, for it promises and strengthens avowed hostility.

Yet conciliation, and nothing less, has been the absurd pretext upon which Sir C. BAGOT has actually promoted to high offices in Lower Canada two open and avowed advocates of separation,— two, we can scarcely credit it while we write it, two open and notorious traitors. *Our* policy is, by conciliating the French population through the loyal and well-affected among them, to make them one with us,—to make them English. Sir C. BAGOT has promoted two men who openly proclaim that *their* policy, their one single object of desire, is to make not the French English, but the English French, —to make, in short, the colony theirs. A more absurd, a more scandalous, and a more suicidal step, so far as hitherto appears, has seldom, we think, been taken by a statesman who calls himself Conservative. . . .

We cannot, however, suppose that these appointments will be approved by the Government at home, nor can we think that the principle on which they proceed is likely permanently to influence the Colonial Administration under the present Ministry. . . . But this is what Canadian politicians call "responsible government": as if the Government of a colony were not responsible to the people of the mother country, as well as to the people of the province. (*The Times*, 18 October 1842)

A further crisis arose in 1844 when Bagot's successor, Sir Charles Metcalfe, experienced difficulties with the LaFontaine-Baldwin ministry over the implications of responsible government, in particular the respective authority of the governor-general and his ministers in making official appointments. Lord Stanley, the colonial secretary, rejected the pretensions of the Canadian ministers to the control of patronage by emphasizing the differences between the position of the governor-general and that of the British monarch.

. . . The hon. and learned Gentleman [Roebuck] had sought to draw an analogy between the position of the Governor General in Canada and that of the Sovereign in this country. He (Lord Stanley) denied the analogy. . . . The Constitution of Canada might be formed upon the model of the Constitution here; but still they could not give to it the life of the British Constitution. . . . The basis of the British Constitution was, that the Sovereign was personally irresponsible for every act of the Government—that the responsibility rested with the confidential advisers of the Sovereign, who were responsible to Parliament and the people for the advice they gave, and he admitted that no Minister could hold permanently the reins of power in this country who did not, in addition to the confidence of the Sovereign, possess the confidence of the popular branch of the Legislature. But because the Crown was not responsible for the acts of Government, the Crown particularly exercised no political power. . . . But the case of a colony was totally different from that of this country . . . the Governor General had none of the dignity of the Sovereign about his position, having an income not more than that of a country gentleman—a stranger to the colony—having probably no personal interest or influence in it until his appointment, and previous to his arrival no connection with it. Place that Governor and the Legislature so constituted in the position of a Minister being himself responsible, and compelled to act in every respect with Parliament, stripped of all real power and authority, liable to act under the control of the leading politicians and parties of the day, and what would they institute in Canada? . . . He said to the hon. and learned Gentleman that he proposed a course which, by no gradual steps, but certainly and at once would place the whole authority in the hands of the dominant party for the time, and convert Canada into a republic, independent of the Crown of this country. It was inconsistent with monarchical Government that the Governor who was responsible, should be stripped of all authority and all power, and be reduced to that degree of political power which was vested in the constitutional Sovereign of the country. Not only would such a course be inconsistent with monarchical Government, but also with the colonial dependence. . . . (*Hansard*, 3rd Series, LXXV, 30 May 1844, 40-42)

The practical implications of responsible government were not fully accepted by the British government until after Earl Grey had appointed Lord Elgin governor-general in 1846. Initially there was much speculation in England whether Elgin would publicly endorse what the *Morning Herald* in 1847 distinguished as the radical or the conservative interpretation of responsible government.

. . . For some twenty years the question of "responsible government" has divided the colonial politicians of British North America; and as both parties appropriate to themselves these watchwords under a different interpretation, each looked with interest and anxiety to the first public exposition of political sentiment made by Lord ELGIN. . . . This question—highly theoretical in its construction, but in its elementary nature eminently characteristic of the political philosophy discussed in a young country—lays bare the very foundations of colonial superintendence, and constitutes the monster difficulty of the British Governor. The Radical's interpretation of his own war-cry is, that every member of the Executive Administration, except the Governor, should be responsible to the Canadian people, dependent upon the popular voice for his official existence, and subservient to the provincial public in every act of his ministerial existence; while the Governor himself, like a mere puppet, should neither by word or deed, countenance or manners, betray his own individuality, but that every petty appointment should be made by his ministerial advisers, and that he himself should be responsible to the Imperial Government in the mother country for acts over which he was not allowed to exercise the slightest control. On the other hand, the doctrine of "responsible government" received by the Conservatives of Canada acknowledges that the colonial Cabinet ought to enjoy a majority in the Provincial Parliament, or resign their offices to men in whom that assembly confides; but it justly vindicates the independence of the Governor as a representative of the British SOVEREIGN and an agent of the British Government; it regards his Excellency as invested jointly with some of the prerogatives of Majesty and much of the independence of the First Minister of the Crown, but wisely leaves to the pressure of circumstances or to individual tact and discretion the amount of initiative influence which he may feel called upon to exercise, and seeks not to rob the representative of the SOVEREIGN of that voice in the disposal of patronage with which his station naturally invests him. At the same time it fully recognises the obligation imposed upon every governor to practise the ennobling duty of softening asperities, mediating between political opponents, and combining for the public service the energy and talents which party spirit would only pervert or monopolise. . . .

. . . a man of Lord ELGIN'S temper and time of life is not likely to barter the prerogatives of the Crown for a short-lived colonial popularity. The very first impartial appointment made by his lordship, will bring the bulldogs of party warfare upon him, and will explain to him practically that in the eyes of the colonial Radicals "responsible government" means the utter surrender of every kind of patronage, large and small, to party purposes, the complete subservience of all imperial interests to colonial prejudices, and the thorough sacrifice of all personal dignity in the Governor on the altar of popular caprice. In the concession of any such principle, the mother country is largely interested, and may be grievously compromised; while the attempt thus practically to wrest the government of a colony from him who is styled its Governor, deserves exposure and reprobation at home, where alone it can meet with effectual counteraction. (*Morning Herald*, 23 March 1847)

Elgin and Grey were determined to adopt the more liberal interpretation, and the issue was effectively settled in 1849 with the British government's confirmation of the Rebellion Losses Act. This proposed to compensate those residents of Lower Canada at the time of the rebellions who had suffered damage to property or other losses through the activities of loyalist volunteers or British troops. Despite protests and demonstrations by English settlers in Canada who objected to compensating those who had openly or tacitly supported rebellion, the imperial authorities sanctioned the act as a matter of purely local concern and as a measure of a ministry possessing the support of a majority in the assembly. The press in England was sharply divided over the issue. The Tory *Morning Herald* and the Whig *Morning Chronicle* denounced the measure and feared its implications for the future of the empire in North America, while the liberal *Globe* considered the act as a local question and strongly criticized the partisan character of the opposition to it.

. . . It is not fair to the Crown to trifle with its colonial possessions until disaffection threatens their dismemberment from the empire, and at the last moment to secure their integrity by heaping favours on rank traitors, who have proved a title to nothing better than the gallows.

Free-trade legislation has paralysed the exertion and straitened the means of the taxpayers of Canada. . . . Poor as the people of Canada are, a law has been passed with a view of taking from the industrious and obedient a portion of the little yet left to them, in order to bestow it upon individuals who, without affection for their SOVEREIGN, or attachment to the institutions under which they live, have contrived, through patronage at home, to obtain the upper hand, and to assist their convicted confederates at the expense of the orderly and well-behaved. Impoverished by free trade—ground down by an excessive public expenditure—the loyal Canadians are called upon to pay rebels taken in arms for the losses incurred by their act of rebellion; having shed blood in defence of the Throne, they are summoned to part with what remains of their substance, in order to compensate all who suffered in their pockets whilst attempting to bring that Throne to the dust. . . .

It is easy to smile at agitations for the repeal of the union existing between Great Britain and any one of her many possessions. It is not difficult to exhibit profound contempt for the efforts of a press directed against the omnipotent hand of the Imperial Government. A wise Minister, however, in the present temper of the world, and in the perilous condition of one and all of the British colonies, will respect the roused anger of a whole community, and give heed to the warnings of journals which do but reflect the public mind. Canada at this moment has nothing to gain from a longer connection with this country. She has everything to hope from alliance with a neighbouring republic, only too eager to welcome and receive her.

Canada will not transfer her loyalty alone and unaccompanied. . . . The example of desertion once given, where will it end? England, bereft of her colonies, and what becomes of her boasted strength and glory? . . . (*Morning Herald*, 21 September 1849)

. . . it may be said that this is purely a Canadian question, and that responsible Government involves, as a matter of course, the acquiescence of the Executive in the proceedings of the representative body, with respect to all such subjects. But, clearly, even according to the extreme theory of responsible government, the Executive has its privileges as well as the representatives—the head of the Government, as well as his Ministers. . . . We must add, however, that this question is, by its very nature, excepted from the category of those to which the principle of responsible government for colonies applies. It is *not* a purely Canadian question—but one which deeply involves the honour of the Imperial Crown, and the authority of the Imperial laws. If Canada were formally independent, she could, of course, do what she pleased with her resources, and might sanction any principles of government that suited her; and we are not prepared to say, that a deliberate sanction, by the Canadian people, constitutionally appealed to, of Mr. LAFONTAINE'S Resolutions, might not be considered as a symptom of fundamental incompatibility between the mother-country and the colony, and as a signal, therefore, that the proper time had arrived for their separation. But that separation has not *yet* taken place. We have relations with Canada, not only formal, but real; not only are her laws administered in the name of our SOVEREIGN, but we are maintaining an army of 6,000 men to defend her against foreign war and domestic disaffection; and, while this is the case, we deliberately say, that it is *impossible* for us to acquiesce in a measure by which the sanction and approval of the Canadian Government are given (in the shape of pecuniary rewards) to rebellion against the QUEEN'S authority, and resistance to the QUEEN'S troops. . . . (*Morning Chronicle*, 22 March 1849)

No one can be astonished at the outrageous fury with which the Canadian Tories have resented the Rebellion Losses Bill, nor at the sympathy they meet with from a portion of the English press. Those politicians and their organs consistently execrate the results of a policy which they long-ago deprecated as inapplicable to a dependency. It has uniformly been the creed of Sir ALLAN McNAB and the old "Family-Compact" men in Canada, that a colony cannot

be ruled by those usages of party-government which work beneficial-
ly in the mother-country; that if constitutional forms are employed
at all, it should only be as a decorous veil for the absolute supremacy
exercised by the Governor of the province, and that the latter can
wisely select his instruments only among a small class, who from
distinctions of race, of social position, or traditional family antece-
dents, are popularly identified with the idea of loyalty to the Crown,
and habitual resistance to the demands of the Colonial *plebs*. . . .

. . . a perseverance on the part of the Home Government in the
practice of Constitutional Legislation will by degrees educate every
party in British North America to the degree of sobriety, patience,
and self-control, which is at once a necessary condition and an
inevitable consequence of freedom. The present outbreak is only a
demonstration, rather more violent than usual, of the strong dislike
which the ex-officials entertain for the practices of Parliamentary
Administration. They naturally make their chief assault on Lord
ELGIN'S refusal to support them with the Royal Veto, which, in the
good old times, had been held the normal weapon and the unobjec-
tionable resort of authority. Mr. ROEBUCK, on the other hand, sees
that Lord GREY has finally secured Canada in the exercise of responsible government. . . .

. . . Here, at all events, is an instance in which Responsible
Government has had full swing. It is impossible that the Canadian
could have been made a more perfect transcript of the British Constitution. . . . (*Globe*, 18 May 1849)

III THE FUTURE OF BRITISH NORTH AMERICA

1. Separatism Considered

At least until the 1840's, Englishmen tended to contemplate the future of the British empire with varying degrees of pessimism and re-
signation. Although some Tories and military men who championed
the cause of colonial possessions professed an unshakable confidence in
the future, such optimism was seldom publicly expressed by writers
and politicians. Before the adoption of free trade and local self-government as the new basis of imperial relations, there was considerable
uncertainty whether it would be possible to preserve the unity of the
empire on some basis other than that of military force, once settlements overseas reached a degree of maturity and self-consciousness

and aspired to govern themselves. The earlier experience with the American colonies led many Englishmen to believe that settlement colonies would eventually declare their independence from Britain, and that the most that could be done in the face of this inexorable tendency was to delay the inevitable and ensure that separation was completed in a spirit of good will. Reflections on the imperial connection in North America were naturally stimulated by the Canadian rebellions, and the following extracts from parliamentary speeches on the Canadian crisis indicate the varying attitudes of politicians to the wisdom and feasibility of preserving British rule in North America. Lord John Russell, for example, was not confident about the future of the empire, but he strongly opposed the idea of abandoning Lower Canada with a precipitate grant of independence.

. . . I come now to a question which has been argued in a very different temper—it is the question whether it is for our interest to abandon Lower Canada altogether. I say, at once, I cannot bring my mind to the conclusion that it would be so. I say at once, that the single motive of the attachment of a considerable portion of the population to the British constitution, and the situation in which they would be left if we abandoned the province to the French party, that single motive would be a sufficient reason with me for emphatically saying "No" to such a proposition . . . there are other considerations which would induce the Government to oppose any project of abandonment. Supposing the St. Lawrence under the command of the United States, and a Canadian republic established at Quebec, does any one believe that the other provinces, the provinces of Nova Scotia and New Brunswick, could be kept under control? . . . the question would arise, whether we should not try to regain Lower Canada, or abandon North America altogether. Is England prepared for such an alternative? I do believe that the possession of our colonies tends materially to the prosperity of this empire. On the preservation of our colonies depends the continuance of our commercial marine; and on our commercial marine mainly depends our naval power; and on our naval power mainly depends the strength and supremacy of our arms. . . . Although, I repeat, that I am not prepared to give immediate independence, this I will say, that if the time were come at which such an important change might be safely and advantageously made, I should, by no means, be indisposed to give the 1,400,000 of our present fellow-subjects who are living in the provinces of North America a participation in the perfect freedom enjoyed by the mother country. If it were a fit time, if circumstances of all kinds were such as to render such an arrangement desirable, I think that our colonies might with propriety be severed from us, and formed into a separate and distinct state, in alliance, offensive and defensive, with this country . . . if the time for such a separation had arrived, (which I utterly deny) we should then have as allies men influenced by the most amiable and affectionate feelings towards the mother country; not men who would wish to see the British arms defeated, or who would entertain the aspiration that the power of Great Britain might sink into insignificance and contempt. . . . (*Hansard*, 3rd Series, XL, 16 January 1838, 34, 41)

Sir Robert Peel, the Tory leader in the House of Commons, echoed these sentiments.

. . . Was this great country prepared to say, on the first manifestation of any rebellious feeling, "Separate from us, and establish a government for yourselves", instead of re-calling them to their duty? He thought not; and that the application of this principle was perfectly inadmissible. . . . In considering the case of Canada, however, it must be inquired what would be the effect on the interests of those colonies in its immediate neighbourhood. If it could be foreseen that on the Canadas becoming independent they would be unable to stand against the United States, and on the first *bona fide* quarrel with them might fall to them, and be annexed to their other territories, and our own British American colonies should thus be separated from each other, we should still be bound by the obligation owed, not only to them, but to other parts of the British empire, to consult their interests. . . . Unless by the strongest circumstances England was compelled to give up Canada, it ought never to permit that country to establish itself as an independent state; and if they should permit that to be done, what answer could be made to the complaints of the other colonies, which would be placed in a subordinate position by the very act of the Government by which they should be protected. He therefore said, that the case of Canada was not a simple abstract question. . . . The situation of Canada and the physical condition of the other colonies of this country in North America must be considered together. That House and the

Government must only look at Canada as an independent state when the situation of the other colonies in America could be regarded as independent states. These were prepared, however, to perform all their duties to this country as colonies, and therefore it would be the grossest folly on the part of England to allow the connexion to be lightly broken. He repeated, then, that the question of the separation or independence of Lower Canada could only be considered at the same time with the navigation of the St. Lawrence, the peculiar circumstances of the other colonies in America, and their neighbourhood to the United States. . . . (*Hansard*, 3rd Series, XL, 16 January 1838, 71-73)

Despite some diversity of views, most of the radicals in parliament tended at this time to favour separation for the North American provinces if this could be amicably accomplished. William Warburton, for example, urged the early adoption of a comprehensive plan for the emancipation of all the British colonies in North America.

. . . When he [Warburton] said, "Emancipate your colonies", he did not mean that this course should be adopted in a hasty or partial manner, but that we ought maturely to consider by what steps we might make that emancipation comprehensive, and include not only Lower Canada, but all the American colonies at the same time, so as to form all into one great federal union. Various objections had been thrown out to his plan for the emancipation of the colonies. First, it was said, "the time is not yet come for such a change; the Canadians do not themselves wish for it; and so far from having any desire to part from the mother country, they are warmly attached to it". Was it their intention, then, to delay emancipation until disaffection proved the real wants of the Canadians? Was it not, on the contrary, most desirable to bring about this change whilst a good feeling towards the mother country still existed? Why not yield to policy and justice what would be forced in the end by extensive disaffection. "Oh, but the colonies do not desire separation; they express no wish for it!" Why, for a very good reason. If any person in the colonies were now to express such an opinion, he would be branded by the loyal party as a traitor. . . . Then the hostility of races and difference of origin, and the necessity of considering and discussing the questions arising out of those circumstances had been adduced as an argument against separation. He admitted it might be an argument against immediate and hasty separation, without due natural regard for the inhabitants of the colonies . . . but this jealously had arisen from the undue favour which had been shown one race, and the state of degradation and submission in which this country had kept the other. . . . In the United States of America, where every race was to be found, but existing under equal laws, no jealously was to be found. People living under equal laws did not employ themselves in cutting each other's throats. . . . While there was still a great remnant of affection for the mother country, if they would determine on a separation, and bargain for the titles of the British settlers, every jealousy and unkind feeling of one to the other would perish. . . . (*Hansard*, 3rd Series, XL, 25 January 1838, 480-1)

The adoption of free trade and the acceptance of local self-government in Canada in the 1840's profoundly influenced contemporary attitudes to the future of the British empire, though diverse conclusions were drawn from these developments. Some Englishmen maintained that the withdrawal of the traditional economic and political bonds of empire would result in its disintegration, and they viewed this probable outcome with pleasure or regret. Others believed that the removal of unwelcome restrictions would assuage colonial discontent and allow full play to the intangible ties of kinship and sentiment between Britain and Canada as a more lasting basis of imperial relations. This confident, optimistic view was expressed by the *Standard* in 1844.

. . . We do not disguise it that we entertain the most sanguine hopes of the perfect conciliation of Canada, and of the complete consolidation of the British Colonial empire, not for a season, as some imagine, but *for ever*. The analogy of all past times is fallacious, because the true principle of colonial government is the discovery almost of yesterday; it is, as Sir Robert Peel expressed, in terms that cannot be improved, "to govern the colonies as if they were integral parts of England". So governed, the colonies will, with all the advantages of political youth, and a wide field for enterprise and industry, have to support them the resources and the power of the wealthiest and the most powerful empire on the face of the earth; and all that will be asked from them is to promote their own prosperity and happiness to the utmost extent possible. How different is this from the old colonial policy which treated colonies as mere tributaries, to be taxed by the metropolitan state at its pleasure, and for its own exclusive profit, or to be bartered away to foreigners in political compromise. Discontent will of course grow up now and then in colonies as elsewhere, but we predict that they will never again extend to the desire of separation. (*Standard*, 25 November 1844)

Some of the most vigorous criticism of colonies and the imperial connection came from Richard Cobden and other radicals who advocated free trade and a reduction in colonial expenditure. Retrenchment was a powerful argument employed by Cobden, but his comments in 1849 suggest that he was not implacably opposed to a reformed empire united by ties of sentiment.

. . . My doctrine for the colonies is this—I would give to our countrymen abroad the fullest amount of self-government they can possibly claim. . . . If people tell me that I want to dismember the empire and abandon the colonies, I say I want Englishmen who are free to possess them. Now, I shall be told that I am going to leave the connexion between the mother country and the colonies of so frail and fragile a character that it will surely be severed. Well, I admit that the political connexion between the colonies and the mother country must become less and less strong, and ultimately I can see that it will be but a mere thread of connexion, politically speaking. But, on the other hand, by giving the colonies the right of self-government, with a right good will shaking hands with them; you will retain the connexion commercially and morally far more strongly than you could by any political bond; the one is by the sword, the other is by the strong bond of affection for the mother country. . . . (Cobden's speech at a public meeting in Bradford, 20 December 1849, reported in *The Times*, 24 December 1849)

While criticisms of overseas possessions, and especially complaints about colonial expenditure, persisted throughout the 1840's, some commentators felt that these views did not reflect the true opinion of the English people. The masses were usually silent and inarticulate but the average Englishman was thought to cherish a deep affection for colonies. A writer in the *Colonial Magazine* in 1849 commended this latent imperial sentiment when he asserted that the critics of empire constituted a small, unrepresentative minority.

> . . . Can it be said that the country is indifferent to the preservation and extension of her colonies? To this supposition, if we would believe the language and literature of the day, we must answer in the negative. It seems to us that not only the national feeling is in favour of preserving what has been already acquired, but that there is an incessant demand for the formation of new establishments. There is, undoubtedly, a small sect, who have mistaken popular arithmetic for political economy, who avow a belief that colonial possessions are useless in peace and dangerous in war, and who are prepared to leave emigration to chance and the colonies to any one who may be pleased to take them. We cannot, however, follow these gentlemen in adopting *Laissez faire* for our motto, or the multiplication table for our creed. We do not anticipate the time when these opinions will spread beyond the clique. They are essentially antinational. History records no instance of a great people being reasoned out of their empire and their traditions by any arithmetical process, however ingenious . . . there is no prospect of our being induced to abandon our dependencies, either from fear of foreign enemies, or for the sake of small economies. . . . ("A View of the Art of Colonisation", *Colonial Magazine*, XVI, May 1849, 308)

The Times developed this theme in 1849 and deprecated the extent to which popular attitudes to colonies could be influenced by appeals to retrenchment and the reduction of taxation, which hardly did justice to the issue in question or to the real sentiments of Englishmen.

> In Mr. WAKEFIELD'S book on the "*Art of Colonization*" there is an interesting and thoughtful chapter on the accession which accrues to the influence and respectability of a country from the number and character of its colonies. . . . From this doctrine Mr. COBDEN and Sir W. MOLESWORTH will of course dissent. The one believes in the approximate dawning of the day when hatred, envy, jealousy, fear, ambition, and spite, are to disappear from national characters and national counsels; when all the world is to be governed by the grand maxim of buying in the cheapest and

selling in the dearest market. Sir W. MOLESWORTH, though of less ready faith, shares Mr. COBDEN'S opinions as to the inutility of colonies. But, bating these distinguished exceptions, the doctrine is, we believe a popular one. Here and there a formidable bill for the government of our dependencies in the shape of army or navy estimates may justify a grumble and provoke a growl. But, despite this, we are convinced that in every society of educated and thinking Englishmen the vast majority would give their vote for the retention, and against the abandonment, of our colonies.

Now, if this be so, it is the duty of every statesman who values that *prestige* which is a real source of power to England, to justify such a sentiment by his own colonial policy. Let him, whether in office or in Parliament, do his best to make the colonies of England serviceable to the honour and greatness of England, in their widest capacity. We have fallen upon parsimonious days and economical tongues. The value of everything is tested by what it will bring ostensibly and directly. Its money cost is narrowly and grudgingly scanned; its prospective profits sceptically weighed. In no cases more than colonial ones. Few people have had reason to take an interest in *them*; but no people are indifferent to taxation. This comes home to their business and bosoms. Talk to them of the imperial fruits of possessing Canada and Australia,—you might as well talk to them about a contingent remainder in the planet Neptune. But talk to them about knocking off an obnoxious tax, and reducing the public expenditure at home, and you have struck upon a chord which responds to every feeling of family comfort and personal enjoyment. To a certain extent this is natural and rational. But it is more general than under the existing conditions of England and her territories it ought to be. Had our colonies always been regarded by our public men as integral parts of the British empire, —differing only from Cumberland, Lothian, Caithness, or Londonderry in their distance from the metropolitan capital,—and had we always exerted ourselves to bring them within the sphere of central contact and the influence of central civilization, we should not now have to lament our late and imperfect performance of a great duty, or to justify the expense which its conditions entail. . . . (*The Times*, 22 March 1849)

Both supporters of empire and its critics, however, came to appreciate the need for colonial reform. The *Standard* developed this point when it argued in 1838 that a policy based on assimilating colonial institutions and society to those of the mother country represented the most effective long-term preparation for independence and the best way to mitigate the existing disadvantages of dependent status.

. . . we must recur to our formerly expressed opinion, that a time will arrive in the age of every prosperous colony at which it will be impolitic or impossible to exercise a control over it, and that it is the duty of a wise and provident legislature to make the best arrangement in contemplation of that time. The precise stage of colonial advancement at which this time shall have arrived is a point on which men may be a little speculative: we are disposed to place it *very late*: at the period, when the mother country and colony will find equal and reciprocal advantages in separation; but surely it will not be denied when a colony has outgrown its parent state in population and resources, and shall have equalled it in influence upon the government of the whole empire, that time has arrived—otherwise the parent state becomes a dependent upon its colony. But though the event is late, preparation for it cannot be begun too early, if, sooner or later, it must come. The task of preparation would be no doubt a difficult one, if the preparatory steps for this future dissolution were repugnant to the measures calculated to ensure present contentment and tranquillity between the respective communities; but the reverse is happily the case. The assimilation of the institutions and of the social condition of the colony, which will secure a perpetual alliance in the independent state, is exactly the process best calculated to ensure a willing obedience of the dependent province while the political connection exists. . . . (*Standard*, 29 January 1838)

Some Englishmen felt that Britain had a responsibility to the colonial empire and a duty to mankind to spread the benefits of civilization which would long outlive a colony's dependent status. This sense of moral responsibility was reflected in the comments of the *Morning Chronicle* in 1848.

. . . "Upon our colonial policy during the next ten years will probably depend the question whether the British Empire is to sink or swim." We have repeatedly urged this view, perhaps even *ad nauseam*, upon the public, for we have an earnest conviction of its reality and truth. The magnitude of the interests at stake in our vast colonial empire, the incalculable influence which our treatment of it must exercise, for weal or for woe, on the history of future ages—the reactive effects produced by it upon the social system of these islands—the opportunities which that empire offers, the responsibilities which it involves—all these great considerations, if properly appreciated, can hardly fail, while they oppress the imagination, to stimulate the efforts, of the statesmen into whose hands this matter is given to be dealt with. Successors in character and mission of the old Romans, the Anglo-Saxon race have taken upon themselves, more or less consciously, the task of replenishing and subduing half the world. Indeed, ours is a fairer field, a nobler work, than that of the Romans, for the edifice which we are constructing is not founded on the blood of conquered peoples, nor the ruins of ancient empires. Our war is with the wilderness. Our trophies are the signs and emblems of humanity and civilization. Our business is not to destroy, but to create—not to enslave, but to emancipate—not to extract tributes, but to extend commerce—not to annex foreign countries, but to enlarge our own. But if the work is glorious, the responsibility is heavy; if we have much given to us, there will be much required; all these young nations, that have sprung from our loins, carry with them and transplant the influences which we impress upon them at their departing. Nay, more—our duties do not stop when they are gone. We have not only to watch over their birth, but to superintend and foster their growth; the people of a "new country" require much which an old country alone can supply —the common metaphor involved in the expression "parent state" has necessarily a corresponding reality. The ties, for good or evil, are not broken; the connection remains, and both parties either profit or suffer by it. If we do not discharge the duties of a parent, we cannot help performing the part of a stepmother. If the shadow of our greatness be not benignant and protective, it must be poisonous and blighting. In short, it is right and just that we should be responsible for the progress or for the degeneracy of our colonial dependencies, for they derive from us the elements from which progress and degeneracy result. . . . (*Morning Chronicle*, 27 June 1848)

Although emphasis on glory did not impress the advocates of economy or free trade as an effective argument in favour of empire, many Englishmen argued that colonial possessions added to the prestige and power of Britain. The *Morning Chronicle* in 1849 referred to this intangible sentiment, and also made the important point that many Canadians and other colonists wanted to remain part of the British empire, once they had achieved self-government and eliminated undue imperial interference in their affairs.

. . . we ought to keep our colonies because they like to be kept; because the connexion is not only beneficial, but agreeable to them; because they have a deep-rooted affection for England, and a pride in being connected with her, which it requires years of persevering mismanagement to eradicate, and which, without such mismanagement, would last and grow for ever. It is not only that they wish to enjoy British institutions, but they wish to live under the British flag—to drink the QUEEN'S health—to sing the National Anthem —to exult, as Britons, in historical glories of Britain, and to claim her heroes, poets, and philosophers as their countrymen. Though such a sentiment may appear to mere economists visionary and unreal, we are fully convinced that it constitutes almost the only link which ought to bind together countries situated too far apart for complete political unity—and that it is a link the strength and importance of which those who know human nature best will rate most highly.

We are also for keeping our colonies because they might indefinitely add to the prestige and power of England—to her prestige in peace, and her power in war. At present, indeed, it may be a matter of doubt whether our colonial empire is a source of weakness or of strength—of glory or of shame; but this is only because England habitually sets aside the true objects of colonial dominion, and takes upon herself to interfere with the trade, the legislation, and the patronage of her dependencies—in short, because she chooses to govern them, instead of letting them govern themselves. . . . But if we wisely confined ourselves to the proper functions of a "mother-country"—if we asked for no further subjection than is necessary to ensure Imperial unity—if, following the example of our ancestors, we delegated to our colonial fellow-subjects an unrestrained power of managing their own affairs in their own way, and required of them merely that they should render allegiance to our SOVEREIGN and stand by our side in relation to Foreign Powers—we should enjoy all the benefits of a colonial empire without the cost, the trouble, and the discredit which it now involves. All subjects of difference would be removed, and the natural loyalty of colonists would burn with an intensity of which those who have never left their mother-country can form no idea, while all would remain which is beneficial to either party in the connection—the sentiment of a common patriotism, and the mutual support against common enemies. . . . (*Morning Chronicle*, 19 June 1849)

2. The Threat of American Imperialism

When Englishmen discussed the future of the British empire in North America, they naturally speculated on the activities and ambitions of the United States. There was some fear and much debate about the possibility that the Canadian provinces might join the American Union, either voluntarily or forcibly by annexation, and the effect of such an event on Britain's international standing. Sources of friction that bedevilled Anglo-American or Canadian-American relations were therefore anxiously examined in England. Never was this more the case than when the rebellions broke out in Canada in 1837, since there then seemed to be a real danger that the Americans would intervene on the side of the Canadian rebels. The federal government was unlikely to instigate an invasion, but many Americans living in the states on the border sympathized with the rebels, and recent events in Texas had demonstated how effectively American citizens could take matters into their own hands. When Molesworth spoke in parliament in December 1837, he voiced a widespread concern about the possible course of events in North America.

. . . "I shudder, Sir", said the hon. Baronet "at the idea of the consequences of a civil war with Canada; it would undoubtedly involve this country in a contest with the United States of America: first, it would bring our Government in collision with the Government of the States bordering on Canada, for volunteers by thousands would swarm into Lower Canada from Maine, Vermont, New York, and Kentucky, animated they would be by the love of adventure—animated still more by the desire of driving the last relics of monarchy from North America, tempted likewise by the promises of rich lands, by the possessions of the anti-popular party; in this respect, I say, let Texas be a warning of what we may expect from

America in the event of a struggle for Canada. Though this interference in the affairs of Canada would at first be confined to individual Americans, it would not terminate there; the conduct of American subjects would not be passed over unnoticed by our Government; complaints and remonstrances would be made to the Union, and the Union would be called upon to prevent its subjects from bearing arms against our troops; this, even if it were willing to do, it could not effect, for how powerful soever the central government of the United States may be when it goes along with the wishes of the people, it is most feeble when the people are opposed or indifferent to its commands, or when one or more of the sovereign states are desirous of evading its decrees . . . for how anxious soever it may be, from general views of policy, to prevent all interference in the affairs of Canada—all hostilities with this country—yet its people will see in this struggle, but a repetition of their own glorious struggle for independence; they will behold in the conduct of England towards Canada the sequel of those despotic and unjust principles which a little more than half a century ago caused them to shake off our yoke—they will rejoice in the triumph of the Canadians, as the great and final victory of democracy in the New World—they will sympathise with their northern brethren as sufferers in the same great cause of liberty; and animated by these noble, these good, and generous feelings, they will take a part in that conflict, which, whatever may be the temporary vicissitudes of war, will never terminate till our dominion in America be for ever destroyed. . . ." (*Hansard*, 3rd Series, XXXIX, 22 December 1837, 1465-6)

Although the Americans might harbour ambitions of acquiring Canadian territory, the *Morning Chronicle* pointed out that, far from being congenial allies, they would give short shrift to the French rebels.

. . . Mr. ROEBUCK, in a letter published yesterday in *The True Sun*, tells the people of England that the Americans will flock into Canada, allured by the bribe of lands. It may not be in the power of the Government of the United States to prevent its citizens from entering Canada any more than from entering Texas. But this we know, the Americans will not submit to the rule of French peasants any more than Englishmen will; and that if they enter Canada they will soon be to the "Nation Canadienne" what the Saxons were to the ancient Britons. The seigneurial rights, the custom of Paris, and all the restraints on profitable occupation so dear to Canadian ignorance, would rapidly under JONATHAN [Uncle Sam] yield to a more sensible system. JONATHAN has a still more thorough contempt for the "Nation Canadienne" than the English have, and he would soon show the Canadians a piece of his mind. . . . (*Morning Chronicle*, 23 December 1837)

Despite some sympathic encouragement for the Canadian rebels, American passions and the border unrest were greatly allayed during Lord Durham's mission, and, as a writer in a journal on colonial affairs reminisced in 1843, the United States government allowed good faith to triumph over latent ambition.

. . . Political fanatics from a neighbouring state were always ready to fan the flame, and thus, luckily for the colony and for Great Britain, an insurrection broke out prematurely, that is to say before the acts of the government in fostering unreasonable expectations in some parties, or assailing the interests or prejudices of others, had materially affected the attachment of the great majority of the people to the crown of Great Britain. The insurrection would in itself have been of no importance whatsoever, so contemptible were its materials for action, had it not been for the political position of the neighbouring countries, and the strong disposition on the part of a powerful body in the United States to incorporate the Canadas with the federal republic.

We do not mean for one moment to charge the executive government of that republic with any sinister design in her dealings with Great Britain at this period; but it must never be forgotten, by those who would form a correct notion of our policy with regard to Canada, that the possession of that territory might be of immense importance to the United States, as it actually is to ourselves; and that, once incorporated with the republic, the ports, the rivers, the minerals contained in British America, would render the United States the most formidable opponent in policy, in commerce, or in arms, that Great Britain ever had to encounter. Canada in short, possesses every advantage that the federal republic does not possess and desires to obtain; and consequently it is perfectly natural that a latent wish,—a hankering, as it is vulgarly termed, for the junction of Canada with the Union, should exist in the breasts of the great majority of American politicians, and equally natural that discontented Canadians should look to such feelings amongst their neighbours as a sure guarantee for support, in case of armed resistance to the authority of Great Britain. . . . ("The Canadas", *Foreign and Colonial Quarterly Review*, I, April 1843, 587-9)

Friction in Anglo-American relations might easily have erupted into open conflict and disputes over territorial boundaries were a potentially fruitful source of discord. One disputed area concerned a particular stretch of the boundary between New Brunswick and Maine where there existed conflicting interests over lumbering and the navigation of the St. John River. In February 1839 hostilities broke out but the crisis soon passed, and the dispute was eventually settled in the Webster-Ashburton Treaty of 1842. English newspapers at the time blamed the Americans for exacerbating the situation by provocative propaganda and urged the British authorities to reject American pretensions. If the Canadas were not to be tamely surrendered, asserted the *Morning Herald* in March 1839, the government should take immediate steps to preserve British honour in the event of war.

. . . With these views, and these feelings pervading the great mass of the inhabitants of the United States, a war between the United States and England is, we repeat, sooner or later, inevitable—unless averted by a policy on our part very different from the present. The pretext for war may be connected with the boundary question, or with any other question which may happen, at the time, to possess a character of convenience, but the object of war on the part of the United States is the annexation of the Canadas to the federal union. War, then, at a moment suitable to the democratic body in the United States, is inevitable—unless England shall assume such an attitude as may render the probable issue of the contest very different from what it appears to be at the present moment. There are but two prudent courses open to this country; the first is, to defend the Canadas, at all hazards, against the attempts of the federal government—and as a guarantee of the integrity of our Canadian possessions, to admit of not the slightest encroachment in reference to the boundary line;—the second is, quietly, and without the cost of an unavailing struggle, to abandon the Canadas. . . . The more prudent course is the bolder course. If the Canadas are worth to the United States (for the question of the boundary line is a mere pretext) a cost of life and of treasure so great, that fifty thousand men, and ten millions of dollars are to be regarded only as the first instalment of the price which our opponents are prepared to pay, what is the worth of the Canadas to England? . . .

The impending struggle with the United States ought, we repeat, to be avoided altogether by the cession of all the claims which the democratic party in the United States may be pleased to advance relatively to the Canadas;—or preparations for the struggle ought, forthwith, to be made, on a scale commensurate with the former greatness of England. . . . If it shall be urged, that England cannot afford to provide such armaments, the reply is obvious—that England cannot afford much longer to retain possession of the Canadas! If we cannot provide the fleets and armies necessary for the maintenance of our colonial power, let us, at all events, turn the "philosophy" of JOSEPH HUME to some account in this, the last, stage of its operation! *Let us sell the colonies*! . . . And let us quietly prepare to take rank, henceforward, amongst third-rate nations! (*Morning Herald*, 28 March 1839)

The attitude of many Englishmen towards the ambitions of the United States and the future of the Canadian provinces was coloured by their fears of the emergence of an overweening rival power. Earl Grey's letters to Lord Elgin in the late 1840's reflect these sentiments, though the colonial secretary was powerless to strengthen Canada's security in the face of demands for retrenchment in England.

. . . I cannot but look forward with great apprehens[io]n as to the future when I see the United States rising so rapidly in power & in population, while at the same time it appears that this giant's strength becomes daily less subject to the restraints of conscience & a respect for right & justice & more entirely at the disposal of the most unscrupulous of mankind. I have always been convinced that this Mexican War w[oul]d create an appetite for the excitement & gain which it has been the means of securing for some of the worst of the Americans which must become very dangerous to the world & especially to ourselves who are placed in such immediate contact with what I must call this detestable people. These considerat[io]ns point out to us the extreme importance of making every effort to strengthen our posit[io]n in N. America, since to have our colonies swallowed up in the Union w[oul]d be to add fearfully to its powers of mischief. With this view the general line of policy you propose to pursue is I am sure the only wise one; you cannot throw too completely upon the Canadians themselves the task of protecting their own lives & properties from all internal disturbance, whilst against aggress[io]n it is our business to protect them. . . .

Against irregular hostilities I trust you have sufficient means of protecting yourself, but I feel that there is too much ground for the American boast that they can take possess[io]n of Canada whenever they please, & I am most anxious to encrease our means of defence. For this purpose there is of course nothing so important as to satisfy the Canadians that it is greatly for their interest to maintain their connect[io]n with us . . . so far as their material interests are concerned it is clear that the Canadians w[oul]d only lose by separat[io]n, which w[oul]d subject them to the high customs duties of the U.S. instead of the very moderate ones they now pay, & I sh[oul]d say that in every other respect they w[oul]d equally be losers by the change, nor do I know what more we can possibly do to convince them of this. But I think it is highly expedient to encrease if we can their power of resisting the overwhelming torrent which the large populat[io]n & great military resources of the U.S. w[oul]d enable them to pour in over so long & open a frontier. Unfortunately everything we could do with this view w[oul]d cost money, & in the present temper of this country money is what we cannot command. . . . (Earl Grey to Lord Elgin, 6 September 1848, Elgin Papers, Public Archives of Canada, MG24.A16)

Some Englishmen suggested that the expansion of American power and republican institutions could be most effectively checked by the creation of a federation amongst the British provinces and by the development of a Canadian national consciousness. J. A. Roebuck urged this view in a letter to Lord John Russell in 1837.

. . . Looking at the American Continent, I see there a power already gigantic. The United States of North America, already possess so large a territory as to render their future increase of dominion a fearful subject of consideration. A few years hence, and all Europe will distinctly feel the preponderating influence of this rising republic. She will quickly be too powerful to be just. No matter how wisely fashioned may be her institutions, how just her laws, her citizens are human beings, and they like the rest of mankind when so powerful as to be above responsibility, will quickly be tyrannical. Her navies will like the armies of ancient Rome, extend the dominion of a proud republic over a prostrate world, while the very intelligence of her people will render them formidable to mankind. Give this nation, the navigation of the St. Lawrence, stretch their dominion over the whole or nearly the whole of the vast continent of North America, and they will while unapproachable themselves, be able with deadly efficacy to attack and to injure the rest of the world. Create a check to this power by making the St. Lawrence the frontier of its dominions, and by laying the foundations of a northern confederation of States, formed of our present North American possessions, and you give mankind the best human guarantee for the moderation and peaceful habits of the United States. The time must come, I do not say that it is come when our present colonies will be independent States, and our conduct now will decide whether, they are to be added to the already too formidable United States, or form another and separate confederation. If we be wise we shall carefully prepare them for this latter condition, and though the chief and first purpose I have in view is to give peace to Canada, one great object of my present proposal is to induce your Lordship to take the first steps towards creating of a balancing power to the American Republic. By so doing so far from hastening the separation of the colonies from the mother country, you will strengthen their union, and lay the foundation for a lasting and amicable relation. . . . (J. A. Roebuck to Lord John Russell, 1837, Roebuck Papers, VIII, Public Archives of Canada, MG24.A19)

The idea of federation continued to be entertained intermittently by imperial statesmen as a future goal of British policy in North America, but, as the comments of Earl Grey in the late 1840's suggest, the time did not yet appear to be ripe for the achievement of this objective.

. . . Lord John [Russell] in a letter I had from him yesterday expresses a good deal of anxiety as to the prospects of Canada & reverts to the old idea of forming a federal union of all the British Provinces in order to give their inhabitants something more to think of than their mere local squabbles, & he says that if to effect this a separation of the two Canadas were necessary he sh[oul]d see no objection to it; his wish in forming such a union w[oul]d be to bring about such a state of things that if we sh[oul]d lose our N. American Provinces they might be likely to become an independent state instead of being merged in the Union—If you remember before you went to Canada we agreed in entertaining an opinion not very different from this as to what is desirable, but on your reaching the other side of the Atlantic you found a state of things wh[ich] you described as rendering the contemplated union at all events premature & making the construction of the projected railway a necessary preliminary to such a measure, since without such an improvem[en]t in the means of communication the physical obstacles to the working of any federal authority w[oul]d be almost insuperable . . . the construction of the railway from Quebec to Halifax . . . w[oul]d at all events be of the greatest importance & contribute more than anything else we c[oul]d do to bind the Colonies to each other & to the Mother Country. . . . (Earl Grey to Lord Elgin, 8 August 1849, *The Elgin-Grey Papers*, 1, 437)

. . . As to the Union of the Provinces—I am sure that this is not a matter to be pressed forward in a hurry, all that can be done is to throw out the general idea & to endeavour by degrees to lead men's minds in that direction; but that *some* bond of union or other ought to be established amongst the different Provinces of N. America I have no doubt whatever supposing it to be practicable—Whether that union ought to be a Legislative one or only federal & in the latter case whether it ought to be more or less complete, are all questions the answer to which must mainly depend upon the state of public opinion when any measure of the sort is attempted. . . . (Earl Grey to Lord Elgin, 2 June 1847, *The Elgin-Grey Papers*, I, 37)

The Traditional
Interpretation:
Seeley to Schuyler

In a survey of historical writings concerning English attitudes to British North America in the period 1822-49, it would be impossible to cover comprehensively the large number and wide variety of books and articles that relate to some aspect of the topic. Part 2 concentrates on those writers and studies which have greatly contributed to the historiography of the subject, and whose explanations and conclusions have been adopted as the basis of more general accounts of the period. Until very recently, there has, in fact, been considerable uniformity in the views of historians writing about English attitudes and policies towards British North America during these years, whatever the nationality of the individual author or the degree of his involvement in this particular period or topic.

The objectives of Parts 2 and 3 will be to examine the characteristics of the major historical writings on the subject, to elucidate their strengths and weaknesses, and to indicate the changing pattern of interpretation. It will be seen that historians have often considered the value, nature, and future of the empire with reference to settlement colonies generally, or the empire at large, rather than with British North America exclusively in mind. Moreover, throughout the following survey, the period from 1822 to 1849 has to some extent been examined within the context of the whole nineteenth century. Some departure from the strict chronological limits of the years 1822-49 has been necessary, because historians have traditionally regarded the development of the British empire from the time of the American Revolution to the emergence of the modern Commonwealth as an evolutionary process that could be divided into certain distinct periods according to the prevailing character of English opinion or policy towards the colonies. Furthermore, the attitudes held in the second quarter of the nineteenth century become more intelligible if set against a broader canvas which indicates how far this era differed from what came before and after.

Unlike the historiography of many issues, this discussion will not show a sharp clash of divergent interpretations or a frequently fluctuating pattern of historical explanation. What can be seen is the creation and consolidation of a traditional, accepted interpretation of British attitudes to empire in the nineteenth century, which writers have begun to question only in recent years. Despite a certain similarity in the views they presented, historians have adopted varying approaches to familiar events, and have emphasized different aspects and contemporary opinions. A historian's particular point of view depends considerably on the sources canvassed and the use made of documentary and secondary material. Evidence may be selected to confirm an author's preconceived explanations, and it may not fairly reflect the contemporary attitudes or developments he purports to study; contradictory evidence may even be ignored. The whole process of selection and composition by the historian is influenced by the preconceptions and values of the individual writer and the age in which he lives. Thus the course of writings on the empire reflects the changing concern of successive generations with continuously relevant issues as the transformation of the empire-commonwealth and the progress of Canadian nationality and unity.

SIR JOHN SEELEY:
THE EXPANSION OF ENGLAND *(1883)*

British imperial history, as a facet of historical inquiry, was a product of the late nineteenth century. It originated with a small but influential group of writers in the late Victorian period whose books and articles on the character and progress of the British empire both reflected and stimulated the growth of a popular imperialist sentiment at a time of increasing international rivalry in the field of colonial enterprise. These writers included politicians, literary figures, and professional historians, the most notable of whom were Sir Charles Dilke (1843-1911), J. A. Froude (1818-94), and Sir John Seeley (1834-95). Their concern over the imperial and international problems which then confronted Britain led them to examine the changing nature of imperial relations. These writings often took the popular form of travel accounts or descriptions of the conditions, resources, and prospects of Britain's colonial possessions, interspersed with personal reflections on the future of the English race and the possibility of preserving imperial unity. But in addition to popular and descriptive narratives, some writings attempted for the first time to examine the development of the British empire and the nature of imperial relations within a distinctly historical context.

The most prominent and influential pioneer of British imperial history was John Robert Seeley, Regius Professor of Modern History at Cambridge University from 1869 until his death in 1895. His views on the British empire were most eloquently and impressively set out in a series of lectures delivered at Cambridge in 1881-2 and published in 1883 under the title, *The Expansion of England*. Although the lectures were nominally concerned with British foreign policy in the eighteenth century, they offered a wide-ranging survey of the rise of the British empire and the character of imperial relations, past and present. The expansion of the empire—the gradual transformation of England into Greater Britain—was presented as the most obvious and momentous tendency in modern English history, though one unaccountably neglected by historians. For three centuries, overseas enterprise in its many forms had profoundly affected the course of Britain's commercial development and foreign relations. The continual discovery, colonization, and exploitation of new continents by the various European states, and the rivalries these imperial interests engendered, had transformed England from an island kingdom, insular in position and outlook, into a leading maritime and colonial power.

In the course of his lectures, Seeley commented only briefly on the attitudes and policies of the early Victorian period. He clearly regarded these years as an unimportant transitional period between the disruption of the old colonial system as a result of the American Revolution and the salutary triumph of free trade some sixty years later. His main reference to the intervening years concerned the appropriate lessons to be drawn from the loss of the Thirteen Colonies. To most Englishmen, the American experience had suggested the inevitable disintegration of an empire once its colonies reached a certain degree of maturity. Seeley felt that the prevalence of this popular belief explained why the growth of the second empire had been regarded with so little interest or satisfaction in the early and mid nineteenth century, and why colonies had then been considered by many contemporaries to be commercially valueless and not worth the effort of retaining. Nonetheless, he thoroughly rejected the view that the American example was universally applicable, or that the tendency towards colonial independence and separation was inexorable.

The reason for his optimism was that he believed that during the course of the nineteenth century an entirely new concept of imperial relations had gradually emerged. Initially, when the defects of the old colonial system had been exposed by the actions of the Americans, Britain did not at once abandon traditional practices. The second empire burgeoned out of the same narrow commercial motives as the first and with the same unsatisfactory system of administration. The conventional attitude, which treated overseas possessions as estates to be exploited, was not effectively modified until the victory of free trade in England symbolized the fall of the old colonial system. The removal of commercial restraints thereafter opened the way for the growth of a new kind of imperial relationship based on ties of kinship and sentiment as British settlers in all parts of the world became increasingly aware of their natural bonds of union.

As a pioneer, Seeley is important in this historiographical survey. His approach to the development of the British empire profoundly influenced subsequent writers, and he gave to imperial history many of its enduring characteristics. Because of his concern with late-Victorian imperial problems, he interpreted the history of the second empire exclusively in terms of Britain's constitutional and political relations with the various overseas settlements. While he condemned the economic restrictions of the old colonial system as a major cause of the American Revolution, Seeley accorded commercial matters a minor and decreasing role in the affairs of the empire once free trade had been adopted by Britain in 1846. Subsequent writers perpetuated this partial, legalistic view of imperial history. Like other commentaries of his day, Seeley's discussion of the nineteenth century empire was largely confined to the settlement colonies: Canada, Australia, New Zealand, and South Africa. Despite some novel comments in *The Expansion of England* on British rule in India, he maintained that Canada and the other white dominions constituted the most vital part of the empire, and this narrow preoccupation was to form the essential core of imperial history in its early years. Moreover, Seeley's predilections led him to view imperial relations entirely from a British standpoint, an emphasis which precluded an examination of colonial interests and of the interplay between local conditions and British policy. Such a myopic and unsatisfactory approach was eventually bound to come under fire from historians in different parts of the Commonwealth, but until that time the lines of inquiry established by Seeley were followed by most early writers on the nature of British attitudes and policies towards the empire.

Seeley's views were based on extensive general reading and reflection, not on painstaking research. The panoramic survey of *The Expansion of England* showed his preference for broad themes and suggestive generalizations rather than for detailed investigation. The thesis of the book was less original than he believed, but he was the first writer to examine this imperial theme extensively and to provide an impressive statement of the prevailing, popular sentiments of his day on colonies and imperial unity. Although its celebrity and influence may have been out of proportion to the originality of its material, the book enjoyed great popularity. Seeley's compelling, reasoned discussion of imperial expansion helped to shape and articulate the views of his own and succeeding generations, and to establish the theme of imperial activity as a major facet of modern British history.

HUGH EDWARD EGERTON: A SHORT HISTORY OF BRITISH COLONIAL POLICY *(1897)*

Although several writers in and prior to the nineteenth century had discussed various phases of British colonial history, the first comprehensive study of the subject was written by Hugh Edward Egerton (1855-1927). Egerton first became interested in colonial affairs when, as private secretary to Edward Stanhope, who served briefly as colonial secretary in 1886, he prepared an official handbook on the colonies for the Emigrants Information Office. Since there appeared to be a need for an authoritative account of the growth of the empire, Egerton devoted his leisure to the study of colonial history. The fruit of his research was *A Short History of British Colonial Policy*, published in 1897 and thereafter frequently reissued and revised. Other books on the empire further enhanced his reputation, and he was appointed to the new chair of colonial history founded at Oxford by Alfred Beit in 1905, a position which he held until 1920.

Egerton's general study, which ranged from early Elizabethan to late Victorian times, was based on extensive research into printed primary sources. For the nineteenth century these principally included *Hansard, Parliamentary Papers*, and volumes of the collected correspondence of leading public figures. Since the book was concerned, as he believed, with the history of opinion, as much as with imperial policy, Egerton allowed statesmen, administrators, and writers to speak for themselves through abundant use of quotations. While this method gives substance and interest to what might otherwise have been a bald summary of events, extensive quotations often take the place of explanatory discussion and analysis of the developments and attitudes being described. Moreover, the diversity of British opinion at any given period is inadequately reflected in the narrow range of individuals whose views are cited as if they were fully representative of contemporary attitudes. An equally significant limitation is that Egerton, too, restricted his inquiry to Britain's relations with the settlement colonies and, somewhat illogically, the West Indies. Nevertheless, within the context of the period at which it was written, his study represents a distinct departure from earlier books on the empire, both in its approach and in its more scholarly use of sources.

In his survey of British opinion and colonial policy in the century following the American Revolution, Egerton discerned four distinct phases. The years after 1783 were marked by despair and disillusion amongst Englishmen as they recovered from the humiliating loss of the Thirteen Colonies. Nevertheless, the period from 1830 to 1860 saw a sudden resurgence of interest in colonies. This revival of imperial sentiment was produced by the influential propaganda and activities of the Colonial Reformers, a group of ardent imperialists amongst whom Egerton included Grey and Elgin, as well as Wakefield, Durham, Molesworth, and Buller. The period was dominated by the movements towards responsible government and free trade. The attainment of these objectives, however, provoked a strong reaction in Britain characterized by the rise of widespread indifference to colonies and what Egerton called "laissez-aller views", which reached their zenith in the 1860's. Nevertheless, anti-imperialist sentiments never commended themselves to the British people generally, and from 1870 onwards a variety of domestic and international developments encouraged Englishmen to reassess the value of colonial possessions and discover a new imperial fervour with the emergence of the empire-commonwealth.

Egerton's account of the years between 1830 and 1860 was entirely preoccupied with the ideas and activities of the Colonial Reformers, which produced an enthusiasm for empire that contrasted sharply with the mood of British opinion both before and after—a theme further elaborated in a lecture delivered by Egerton in 1913, entitled "The Colonial Reformers of 1830", and subsequently published in F. J. C. Hearnshaw (ed.), *King's College Lectures on Colonial Problems* (London, 1913). With the loss of the American colonies the Englishman's natural confidence in empire had been destroyed and considerable doubts cast on the most cherished principles of the old colonial system. With "the decay of mercantilism, the idea of a colonial Empire drifted on the waters, like some ship riddled by its enemies' guns, that floats on a calm sea, ready at the first storm to break up". (p. 175) Since colonies were no longer considered indispensable for trade, and their administration and defence imposed a heavy financial burden on the British taxpayer, it was natural that Englishmen should have wondered whether Britain would not benefit from being rid of such encumbrances. "It was upon this scene of low ideals and practical difficulties that the colonial reformers entered in 1830; and it is not too much to say that at once the imperial horizon was widened, and a return seemed again possible to the spacious days of great Elizabeth." (p. 177) It had also been confidently predicted by contemporaries that history would repeat itself, and when the colonies in British North America and elsewhere reached sufficient maturity, they too would separate from the mother country. Independence was regarded as the inevitable outcome of colonial development, and this process now took on the character of a fixed historical law. "That this natural tendency was arrested, that a new idea of an Empire at once self-governing in its component parts and yet one as against the outside world sprang into being, was due to the work of a small body of men" (p. 150), the Colonial Reformers, who breathed a fresh spirit into imperial relations.

A major part of the campaign conducted by the Reformers was concerned with the advocacy of systematic colonization, by which they proposed to alleviate economic and social distress in Britain. While the benefits and management of emigration had previously been discussed by British politicians and writers, Wakefield's theory and the propaganda of the Reformers inaugurated a new era in which popular attitudes towards emigration were significantly changed and systematic colonization was substituted for the haphazard migration of paupers overseas. Egerton maintained that British statesmen were at least partially converted to Wakefield's ideas after 1830, so that for a short time imperial practice haltingly followed rather than anticipated theory. Public lands in British North America, Australia, and elsewhere came to be regarded as an asset of empire for which British statesmen acted as trustees on behalf of future emigrants and colonists, and Egerton cited the views of Durham and Grey as typical of a more enlightened attitude to land affairs. In the case of Canada, the Durham *Report* effectively exposed the glaring abuses in land administration and the urgent need for new procedures that would better facilitate emigration from the British Isles.

Egerton gave great prominence both to the vigorous criticisms levelled by the Colonial Reformers against the system of imperial administration at home and overseas and to their advocacy of the principle of responsible government. Although he admitted that the bitter attacks of Wakefield and Buller were partisan, he maintained that there was an essential core of truth in their denunciations of the excessive centralization of imperial authority and the bureaucratic rule of irresponsible officials in Downing Street. While there was no overt desire to curtail colonial liberties, discontent in the Canadas during the 1830's could be attributed to defects in the existing form of colonial government, which was 'popular' but not 'responsible', and in which the local executive lacked the necessary vigour and initiative to deal with a demagogic assembly.

Egerton did not believe that the history of Canada during this period represented a precise re-enactment of the old story of colonial emancipation. Lord Durham had correctly diagnosed the struggle in Lower Canada as a racial contest, and this fact rendered the constitutional question of less importance in Upper Canada. Whatever the objections of English settlers to the family compact and its hold over the colonial executive, there could be no question that the great majority of the inhabitants of British North America were determined to preserve the connection with the mother country. Although the state of affairs which culminated in the rebellions of 1837 should not have been allowed to develop, contemporaries were wrong in thinking that the future of the empire was in any way seriously endangered. The unshakable optimism of the Colonial Reformers was fully justified by events.

Egerton strongly criticized the view of some earlier writers that the concession of responsible government was part of a general policy of cutting the colonies adrift and was deliberately granted as a stage on the road towards total separation from Britain. Whatever might have been the secret beliefs and expectations of leading British statesmen, it was impossible to deny that Durham, who first brought responsible government within the range of practical politics, possessed unbounded confidence in the value and permanence of the empire in North America. On every page of his celebrated *Report*, Egerton claimed, there breathed an exceptional passion of imperial patriotism. Moreover, statesmen such as Russell and Grey, who had much to do with the actual introduction of responsible government, were not advocates of separation. While that generation did not possess complete confidence in the permanence of the colonial connection, Egerton believed that it was only when local self-government had been practically achieved in Canada and Australia that Englishmen began seriously to question the value of colonial possessions.

To some extent this further shift in public opinion, which became marked by 1860, reflected both the success and the failure of the programme of the Colonial Reformers. Responsible government weakened the formal political ties that had hitherto been associated with colonial dependency and thus profoundly changed the nature of imperial relations. The Reformers' proposal to divide the fields of administrative responsibility and reserve certain areas for imperial control was found to be unrealistic, because interference by the mother country was possible only in the earlier stages of colonial development. As communities in North America grew to manhood and aspired to complete control over their affairs, these reserved powers had to be surrendered. It was both paradoxical and an indication of their confused optimism that the Reformers should simultaneously have advocated local self-government and continued imperial responsibility for colonial lands, a crucial field of administration which the colonists would want to control. Despite the liberal sympathies of the Reformers, a more realistic and acceptable balance had to be struck between imperial authority and colonial self-government as the basis of Britain's future relations with the dominions.

The change in public opinion concerning colonies after 1850 was more directly influenced by the victory of free trade in Britain. Egerton had little to say about the progress and triumph of this movement, since he regarded it as a facet of English domestic history. Consideration of the colonies or their interests played no part in the struggle against protection, as the fluctuations in British policy over the admission of Canadian wheat into the British market in the 1840's seemed to show. The introduction of free trade in 1846 placed a severe strain on Canadian loyalty, and the fact that Canada did not then join the American Union or separate from the empire reflected no credit on the wisdom of British statesmen.

Although the die had been cast with respect to the general commercial policy of the empire, Englishmen were as yet uncertain how far British theory and practice were to dictate trade regulations in the colonies. Statesmen such as Grey regarded commercial relations as a matter to be controlled by the mother country. Anxious to see the colonists enjoy the benefits of free trade, Grey was certainly not the man to yield when this 'sacred' cause was at stake; thus it was fortunate for the peace of the empire that a more accommodating colonial secretary was in office in 1859 when the issue of commercial policy and its regulation was ultimately raised by the Canadians.

Nevertheless, Egerton admitted that the movement towards free trade profoundly altered both the attitudes of Englishmen to colonial possessions and Britain's relations with them. For almost two centuries, the chief object of European nations in acquiring colonies had been the economic gains accrued from the monopoly of their commerce. But if such monopolies were unsound in theory and led to political independence in practice, it seemed to follow that colonies were not really advantageous to the mother country. The triumph of free trade, allied to the acceptance of responsible government, therefore encouraged Englishmen to question the value of overseas possessions. A general feeling that the separation of the colonies was simply a question of time also began to develop; meanwhile, all that could be done was to ensure that the eventual disruption of the empire took place with cordiality and dignity. These arguments, Egerton maintained, led to the predominance of scepticism and *laisser-aller* views in Britain after 1855; that these sentiments did not emerge before that date could be attributed to the continuing influence of the Colonial Reformers.

Indifference to colonies and *laisser-aller* principles reached their climax, Egerton argued, in the 1860's when tendencies which had long been in the air began to assume a more distinct shape. The origins of this scepticism could be discerned in a much earlier period, and there had been critics of empire and opponents of imperial expansion since the time of the American Revolution. No great stress ought therefore to be placed on the originality or the constant use of such language by Richard Cobden, John Bright, and other politicians of the Manchester school. The important question, Egerton suggested, was to decide how far moderate statesmen had become imbued with separatist views, and he argued that this was not the case until the 1860's when the influence of the Manchester school reached its height. Egerton produced little evidence to support this contention, though it was obviously related to the rise and fall of the Colonial Reformers as the typical representatives of influential radical opinion. Between 1830 and 1850 most English radicals had been advocates of colonial expansion, but, after the death of Molesworth in 1855, the last spokesman of this school, a wholly different type of radicalism predominated and its influence in British politics extended far beyond its nominal supporters. By the 1860's, therefore, the unchallenged ascendancy of the Manchester school had resulted in the triumph of anti-imperialist sentiment in England.

Thus Egerton placed the climax of this mood of anti-imperialism in the sixties and he discerned only slight traces of its existence in preceding decades. Later writers, however, were to antedate the rise of anti-imperialism in Britain and find substantial evidence of indifference and even hostility to colonies at a much earlier period. Egerton confined *laisser-aller* views to the years after 1855, because he regarded them as the long-term product of free trade and responsible government, and because he considered the period 1830-55 as one overwhelmingly dominated by the Colonial Reformers. Subsequent historians modified this interpretation when they examined a wider range of British opinion than Egerton had done and thereby reached the conclusions that scepticism was more widespread amongst Englishmen during these years and that the Colonial Reformers were not so influential or representative of contemporary opinion.

JOHN LYLE MORISON:
BRITISH SUPREMACY & CANADIAN SELF-GOVERNMENT
1839-1954 *(1916)*

Since it was a pioneering work in a new field of historical inquiry, Egerton's book exerted a considerable influence over writers on the empire during the following decades. This influence can be seen in one of the earliest monographs to examine an important facet of Anglo-Canadian relations in the period under discussion. The book by John Lyle Morison (1875-1952), *British Supremacy & Canadian Self-Government 1839-1854*, was published in Glasgow in 1916 when the author was professor of colonial history at Queen's University, Kingston. Between 1901 and 1907 he had lectured at the University of Glasgow, and from 1922 to 1940 he taught at the University of Durham. In 1928 he published a biography, *The Eighth Earl of Elgin, a Chapter in Nineteenth-Century Imperial History*.

In his earlier book on imperial relations, Morison argued that between 1839 and 1854 British statesmen attempted to reconcile within the framework of empire the supremacy of British authority and the Canadian desire for local autonomy. In contrast to the prevailing indifference among Englishmen, a small group of Colonial Reformers provided a possible solution to this dilemma and their ideas were gradually accepted by the British government. But the Reformers wanted to combine local self-government with continued imperial supervision, while the Colonial Office did, in fact, more realistically surrender its remaining authority. This outcome was facilitated by the growth of scepticism in Britain concerning the value of colonies and the preservation of imperial unity that predominated after 1850 with the ascendancy of the Manchester school and *laissez-faire* doctrines.

Morison's book dealt mainly with the course of events during these years and the progress of imperial relations under successive governors-general but, as essential background to the study, one chapter was devoted to an examination of general English opinion on the colonies and of the attitudes and policy of the British government. Although he claimed that a "considerable portion of authoritative British opinion" had been covered (p. 291), Morison, in fact, restricted the range of opinions and sources he thought relevant. It was unnecessary "to exhibit the otiose or irresponsible opinions of men or groups of men, which had no direct influence on events". (p. 231) With this criterion, little needed to be said about the views of the British populace; the attention of the public was directed to Canadian affairs only when rebellions or other sensations occurred, and at all other times it displayed an indifference that was not without advantage to the authorities. The British press could also be discounted, because Elgin and Grey considered it "wonderfully ignorant and misleading on Canadian subjects". (p. 232) The unfair methods of the newspapers were shown, Morison maintained, in their neglect of the real issues in Anglo-Canadian relations and their emphasis on irritating but unimportant disagreements —a charge that is factually untrue. He concluded that "in all political questions demanding expert knowledge, newspaper opinion is practically worthless. . . . Canadian problems owed nothing of their solution to the British press", (p. 233) a naive and unconvincing judgment for someone purporting to examine English opinion on colonies.

As far as Morison was concerned, the only feasible and fruitful starting-point for a discussion of the development of British opinion on Canadian questions was with the Colonial Reformers. The situation following the rebellions of 1837 was especially favourable for the ideas of these radical and unconventional spirits, since a solution was urgently needed to the basic problems of colonial government. Their imaginative scheme envisaged the combination of Canadian autonomy and British supremacy, and unlike their more sceptical contemporaries, the Reformers boldly accepted and championed the apparent contradiction implicit in this formula. On the one hand, they proposed to give the colonists entire control over their domestic affairs. On the other hand, they upheld the right of the mother country to act with complete authority in specific, limited areas of administration. The great merit of Durham and his associates, Morison argued, was that they resolved the theoretical, conceptual difficulties involved in the constitutional position of Canada at this time by overriding them; the Colonial Reformers squared the circle. Furthermore, these noble radicals were distinguished by their confidence in the future of the empire and in the unquenchable affection of the colonists for the mother country. The Reformers' robust and unhesitating imperialism, Morison maintained, stood in sharp contrast to the views of every other political group in Britain and against the general background of conservative restriction and distrust. Their confident imperial note was the most striking contribution of the Durham radicals to colonial development, and the originality and unexpectedness of their confidence gained in impressiveness when contrasted with popular attitudes of the day.

Morison then turned to examine the way in which the views of the Colonial Reformers came to influence the policy of the British government but were transformed by successive colonial secretaries into an experiment distinctly bolder than anything the radicals had planned. In general the bureaucracy of the Colonial Office did not understand the governing of colonies such as Canada; where ministers had the will and ability, they lacked sufficient knowledge to pursue policies that were at once democratic and imperial in character. Even Earl Grey sometimes lapsed from the optimism which the empire demanded of its statesmen. Morison also questioned the common assumption of writers that the permanent officials at the colonial department, in particular James Stephen, exerted a powerful and direct influence over the course of British policy towards Canada. While this may have been true before 1839, Morison refused to believe that Stephen and his bureaucratic colleagues exercised effective influence over such independent and strong-minded secretaries of state as Russell and Gladstone, over an irritatingly conservative individual like Stanley, or over an expert in colonial affairs like Grey. Whatever dominance Stephen might have enjoyed over Glenelg in the late thirties and used to initiate the concession of greater self-government to Canada, his influence must have speedily waned thereafter while the independent intentions of the responsible ministers reasserted themselves. No evidence was produced, however, to substantiate these confident assertions. Once he had thus dismissed as unimportant the views of Stephen and the other permanent officials, Morison considered himself free to concentrate his discussion on the crucial attitudes of Russell, Stanley, and Grey as being synonymous with British colonial policy.

Stanley's administration between 1841 and 1845 required little comment. With an arrogant and unyielding disposition, he administered Canada in a mean, irritating spirit, and with emphasis on the limitations of colonial self-government. All existing evidence proved, Morison claimed, that the leaders of the Tory party opposed a generous interpretation of Canadian rights. The Tories naturally and logically condemned all forms of democratic control, and they stood for the strict centralization of imperial authority. But while they wanted to hold the colonies with a firm hand, such a policy produced colonial discontent and this in turn bred doubts concerning the possibility of retaining overseas possessions by the traditional methods. The Tories therefore accompanied their doctrine of British supremacy and centralized authority with pessimistic prophesies concerning the connection between Britain and the colonies and with talk of separation—a judgment which is certainly not true of the Tory newspapers of the period whose views Morison disdainfully ignored.

Morison thus narrowed the scope of his inquiry to an examination of the attitudes of the more liberal Whig ministers to the nostrums of the Colonial Reformers. While Lord John Russell was not particularly farsighted, he appreciated the existing defects in colonial government. He revised the tenure of crown offices in the colonies in 1839, and did nothing to hinder a movement towards greater local control which he only partially understood. He was prepared to concede a generous measure of internal self-government to Canada, but he felt more acutely than Durham the difficulty concerning the location of ultimate authority within an empire. Morison maintained that between 1841 and 1847 Russell's views were interestingly modified. At first, his liberal sympathies with regard to greater local control were qualified by his belief that the connection between colony and mother country demanded the retention of British supremacy. But he later saw that responsible government was a broader thing than he had initially considered it, and with his genuine sympathy for liberty and democracy he accepted a more complete surrender to Canadian demands. Since this surrender meant a relaxation of British supremacy, however, Russell's confidence in the future of the imperial connection correspondingly waned. By

1847, he was no longer an imperial optimist; but if this change of opinion seemed somewhat to his discredit, Morison cited the similar modification that occurred during these years in the views of Sir Robert Peel on Canada and the empire.

This then brought Morison to Earl Grey, who in 1846 became the dominant influence in colonial policy. In his study of colonial and economic questions, Grey had imbibed many of Wakefield's ideas. During his regime, *laissez-faire* principles were given their fullest expression, as free trade and responsible government became the basis of imperial policy. Grey also believed that the empire redounded to Britain's material advantage and was a potent instrument for the welfare and peace of the world. Separation would not only be unfortunate and degrading for the British, but would also be contrary to Canada's best interests. Morison greatly approved of Grey's statesman-like and noble view of empire, which claimed from the colonists a loyalty proportionate to the generosity of the crown.

Nevertheless, the concluding stage in the evolution of mid-Victorian opinion concerning Canada was dominated by separatist sentiment. Most statesmen during the early years of Victoria had expected that the connection between Britain and Canada would eventually be disrupted. The partisan and reckless use of the term 'Little Englander' by later writers to describe anti-imperialist sentiment, so Morison argued, had largely concealed the fact that all responsible politicians between 1840 and 1860 were moving steadily towards a Little England, sceptical view of the future of the empire. The exceptions were Durham, whose faith was not put to the test of experience because of an early death, and Buller, Grey, and Elgin, who had special grounds for their continued confidence. A pessimistic outlook was natural amongst Tories, especially with the concessions made to colonial demands. As for the Whigs, Morison attributed the growing separatist views to the transformation of the party in the 1840's, as a result of which the doctrines of the Manchester radicals prevailed. Cobden and Bright accustomed the Whigs and Englishmen generally to more businesslike attitudes which questioned the value of colonies, and, as *laissez-faire* became the dominant principle in politics, earlier concepts of imperial supremacy and colonial dependence were displaced.

Morison therefore concluded that, beneath the contradictions and diversity of British opinion, a broad tendency towards a belief in the eventual separation of Canada from the empire could be discerned after 1840. As in commerce the security of protection was abandoned for the doubtful advantages of free trade; so in local government, autonomy had to be conceded. It was not strange that Englishmen should have perceived in this process the signs of disruption rather than the gleams of hope. Yet they failed to appreciate what Morison considered the one really significant factor in the situation—the inclinations of the Canadians. Apart from the Colonial Reformers, who realized that colonists entertained British sentiments and loyalties, Englishmen of that day did not recognize that the connection depended less on what British ministers thought of Canada than on what Canadians thought of the mother country.

Morison's study does not represent a comprehensive picture of British opinion, since the attitudes of too few individuals and groups were examined. He dismisses Englishmen generally as supporters of separatism, though little evidence is produced to substantiate this crucial generalization. The author would no doubt have argued that such criticisms were beside the point, because only the views of leading statesmen mattered in practice, whether or not they were truly representative of their contemporaries. It is debatable, however, whether half a dozen steadfast imperialists did exercise such a decisive influence over the course of events without being affected by, or reflecting the opinions of, ministerial colleagues, professional civil servants, politicians, economists, or the press, all of whom Morison ignores or discounts as unimportant.

A further characteristic of this account is the distinct contrast drawn between the imperial sentiments of a few individuals and the pessimism and indifference that generally prevailed in Britain. This dichotomy became part of the standard view of the period adopted by historians in the early twentieth century, but Morison tried harder than most to place public figures in one of these extreme categories—imperialist or Little Englander. Moreover, this exercise in dichotomy clearly exposed the author's own prejudices. Support for imperial unity, confidence in the empire and its value, Canadian loyalty to the crown—these are the qualities which Morison equates with farsightedness and statesmanship, thus creating a very partial and distorted survey of British opinion.

C. A. BODELSEN:
STUDIES IN MID-VICTORIAN IMPERIALISM
(1924)

The first scholarly monograph to examine in detail British attitudes to empire in the nineteenth century was *Studies in Mid-Victorian Im-*

perialism, written by C. A. Bodelsen, a Danish historian, and published in Copenhagen in 1924. Although the book was principally concerned with the rise of an imperialist spirit in Britain in the later nineteenth century, this popular sentiment emerged in the early 1870's as a protest and reaction against separatist tendencies which seemed so powerful in the middle of the century. Bodelsen therefore began his book with a discussion of the origin and character of mid-Victorian separatism, including a reference to the temporarily influential campaign of the Colonial Reformers. Rather than write an exhaustive account of the progress of the anti-colonial movement, he sought to illustrate it by extracts from the speeches and writings of prominent statesmen and writers, to analyse its various forms, and to explain the foundations on which it rested. His study of British opinion was based on material drawn from an extensive canvass of contemporary literature, parliamentary debates, and some leading newspapers and journals. As was the case with other historians of that day, Bodelsen concentrated attention on Britain's relations with the settlement colonies. This preoccupation was reflected in his essentially political concept of the elusive term 'imperialism', which he defined as "that specifically British movement which aims at preserving and consolidating the unity of the British Empire". (p. 7)

Bodelsen traced the origins of separatist sentiment and British scepticism concerning the value of colonial possessions to the loss of the American colonies. This disillusioning experience persuaded Englishmen that independence was the inevitable destiny of overseas settlements, a belief that was further strengthened by "the cult of liberty in the abstract", one of the chief legacies of the French Revolution. At certain times in the nineteenth century, this ingrained conviction coloured the outlook of most Englishmen to colonial questions and deeply influenced the course of imperial relations. Furthermore, the British North American colonies and other possessions that remained within the empire after 1783, as well as those acquired during the wars with France, were as yet relatively undeveloped and thinly populated. While they might eventually become flourishing and valuable provinces, for the moment their retention in their present immature condition entailed considerable inconvenience and expense. Therefore, from the time of the Napoleonic Wars onwards, many Englishmen began to question the wisdom of continuing to bear the burdens of colonial dependencies, since their connection would be severed as soon as the colonies became mature and useful communities, at last able to offer some tangible return to Britain.

Bodelsen supported these contentions with quotations from a wide range and variety of contemporary commentators. The earliest advocates of separation were the celebrated political economists writing in the late eighteenth and early nineteenth centuries: Adam Smith, Josiah Tucker, Jeremy Bentham, and James Mill. The "early Free-Traders and those of the Utilitarians and the 'Philosophical Radicals' who were not associated with the Colonial Reform Movement had Separatist leanings". (p. 14) To illustrate other and later exponents of this point of view, Bodelsen assembled a random collection of quotations drawn from the years between 1822 and 1840, in which critical or sceptical opinions on the value of colonies and the future of the empire were expressed by an assortment of individuals, including Joseph Hume, Lord Brougham, J. A. Roebuck, Henry Warburton, Sir Henry Parnell, and Lord Ashburton, and by the periodicals, the *Edinburgh Review* and the *Westminster Review*. In this potpourri of opinions, Bodelsen gave no indication of the context in which the comments were made, the specific occasion, or whether the quoted remarks reflected the enduring views of the individuals concerned.

That separatist ideas did not completely predominate in the first half of the nineteenth century could be chiefly attributed to the activities of the Colonial Reformers, whom Bodelsen regarded as the forerunners of late Victorian imperialism. Durham, Wakefield, Buller, and Molesworth were radicals, but theirs was a brand of radicalism entirely different from that which emerged by the mid century with the ascendancy of the Manchester free traders, because it was "inspired by the liberty-worship of the French Revolution (modified to suit English conditions), not by economics". Nevertheless, Bodelsen admitted that even the Colonial Reformers at times expressed views on the empire that bordered on scepticism. "Owing to their devotion to liberty in the abstract, and to the fact that retrenchment occupied a prominent place on the Radical programme, the Colonial Reformers, especially Molesworth, sometimes used language which laid them open to the charge of Separatism." Unfortunately, Bodelsen did not elaborate this very important divergence in the views of the Reformers. "In reality", he was content to conclude, "they were the truest Imperialists of their time, and it is hardly too much to say that it was due to their efforts more than to anything else that the second colonial Empire did not go the way of the first." (p. 16) While their advocacy of systematic colonization was valuable in itself, "Responsible government probably saved the Empire". (p. 18)

Although the Colonial Reformers were a minority, the energy with which they participated in the debate on colonial questions and the prestige which they enjoyed as experts on colonial affairs gave them a considerable influence over contemporary opinion and imperial policy in the thirties and forties. Though they disagreed with the Reformers on many points, statesmen like Russell and Grey, and thinkers like John Stuart Mill, were materially affected by the Reformers' widely publicised ideas. Bodelsen presented no evidence, however, to show precisely in what ways and to what extent the Reformers shaped either public opinion or the attitudes and actions of statesmen, beyond the customary reference to the adoption of responsible government in Canada and Australia and the introduction by the Colonial Office in Australia of some of Wakefield's ideas on colonization. Nevertheless, the heyday of the Colonial Reformers was comparatively shortlived. Not only did the leaders of the movement die young, but events were soon to prove that they had been too optimistic in their belief that local self-government and continued imperial authority in certain reserved fields of administration could be successfully combined in a formula that would provide a permanent basis for imperial relations. Canadians regarded the acceptance of responsible government as merely the first step towards full autonomy, and, as they began to encroach on what had originally been intended as the preserve of the British authorities, one by one the reservations contemplated by Durham came under local jurisdiction. This gradual crumbling away of the remnants of imperial control militated against a belief in the permanence and desirability of the colonial connection. A serious blow was dealt against the popularity of the empire in Britain when the Canadians adopted a policy of tariff protection in the 1850's at a time when a substantial section of the English public was wedded to free trade and regarded protection as little short of criminal or insane. With these developments in the field of commercial relations, it was hardly surprising that Englishmen lost faith in the nostrums of the Colonial Reformers.

As the influence of the Reformers waned, a new brand of radicalism, which was essentially economic in origin and character, came into the foreground. The doctrines by which this middle-class movement was principally guided were those of the Manchester school, whose chief political leaders were Cobden and Bright, and whose most brilliant literary exponent after 1850 was Goldwin Smith. Since the colonial system was associated with the outmoded doctrines of mercantilism,

Bodelsen argued that free-trade and *laissez-faire* principles naturally gave adherents of the Manchester school a strong bias against the retention of colonies. The emphasis which the Manchester school placed on material rather than sentimental considerations, their demand for retrenchment, and their undeniable overtones of pacifism and antimilitarism characterized them as advocates of separatism.

When he came to examine the reasons for the widespread influence of separatist sentiment in Britain, Bodelsen maintained that the victory of free trade in the 1840's removed a major justification for the possession of colonies. While many Englishmen had ceased to value commercial monopolies and restrictions long before the final triumph of free trade, the actual abolition of the preferential system seriously undermined popular belief in the possibility and the advantage of retaining overseas possessions. The colonial connection was commonly regarded as something artificially maintained in opposition to tendencies that would otherwise lead to emancipation. Given the belief that separation was only a question of time, Bodelsen did not find it surprising that Englishmen were disinclined to incur sacrifices, and in particular the substantial expenditure for naval and military defence for the sake of colonies. Moreover, it was suggested that the possession of colonies increased the possibility of Britain's involvement in war, and this argument seemed particularly applicable to Canada, which might at any time become embroiled in hostilities with its powerful neighbour and which would be extremely difficult and costly to defend. Canada therefore became the *bête noire* of the separatists, and attempts to prove the uselessness of dependencies were generally illustrated by references to British North America—a crucial point on which Bodelsen might have usefully elaborated.

Critics of empire also argued that there was little to show in return for this expenditure and inconvenience. Calculated per head of the population, colonies were better customers than foreign countries, but it was impossible to prove that this was not a natural consequence of economic forces that would continue to operate if and when the political connection with Britain was severed. The separatists could point to the substantial growth in Anglo-American trade after the United States became independent. Similarly, when the advocates of empire referred to the usefulness of colonies as outlets for British emigrants, critics could assert that emigration would proceed at exactly the same rate if these territories were to become independent. Such a statement could not be disproved, and in support of it could be adduced the stream of migrants who left Britain for the United States. The question whether the colonies were economically beneficial to Britain seemed the more relevant because the public was inclined to regard the territories of British North America and Australasia as British possessions in the literal sense of the word, a justified view considering that these vast areas were sparsely populated. To the contemporary Englishman, colonies were primarily lands, not people.

Yet separation was not only advocated in view of its advantages to the mother country. Bodelsen pointed out that many critics of empire believed the striking growth in the prosperity and power of the United States to be a product of political independence; thus by retaining the colonies as dependencies, Britain was retarding their material progress and preventing them from realizing a similar success. Apart from purely economic considerations, the state of subjection, believed to be inseparable from colonial status, was also considered adverse to the development of self-reliance and self-respect in overseas communities. In this way the separatists drew their arguments from a consideration of both British and colonial interests.

Once he had discussed the sources of separatist views, Bodelsen proceeded to examine the extent to which these sentiments were accepted by the British public. He emphasized that colonial affairs were generally debated in an atmosphere of indifference and ignorance, except when some spectacular event like the Canadian rebellions momentarily attracted public attention. Few politicians, he believed, took an interest in colonial questions when they were not related to a topic of more absorbing or immediate concern, such as retrenchment or relations with the United States. Bodelsen admitted, however, that it was extremely difficult to determine how far mid Victorian statesmen as a whole were influenced by the teachings of the separatists; few ministers or people in responsible public positions would have expressed a frank desire to be rid of British subjects and possessions, whatever their private convictions. There were of course always statesmen such as Russell, Grey, and Elgin, who firmly believed that the continued unity of the empire was both possible and desirable. But Bodelsen felt that most supporters of empire remained comparatively passive advocates and that they offered no serious opposition to the rising tide of popular separatist sentiment. "On the whole", he concluded, "it may be said that Separatism grew steadily in force from about 1850 for nearly twenty years." (p. 43)

Amongst those who expressed sceptical or critical views on colonies,

Bodelsen distinguished two groups: Separatists proper and Pessimists. A comparatively small group of Separatists thought that the loss of the colonies would be a matter for congratulation, and even advocated taking positive steps to hasten the event. "This group was perhaps not very numerous, but it counted among its members . . . the leading members of the Manchester School (thus exercising a considerable indirect influence on the Liberal party), it was energetic, and knew its own mind, and its influence was consequently out of proportion to its numbers." (p. 43) At the same time there was a much larger group of Pessimists who did not actually rejoice at the prospect of separation, but who considered emancipation to be the ultimate destiny of colonies. Bodelsen admitted that the borderline between these Pessimists and the Separatists proper was somewhat vague, but a belief in ultimate separation coloured the outlook of most Englishmen after the mid forties and made them unwilling to countenance financial and commercial sacrifices by Britain on behalf of the colonies. "This group", he concluded, "probably comprised the majority of mid-Victorian statesmen of both parties." (p. 43)

In his concluding assessment of the character and contribution of early and mid Victorian separatism, Bodelsen criticized later writers for labelling a variety of contemporary opinions influenced by the most widely differing motives as 'separatist', a charge from which Bodelsen himself was not entirely free. In reality, he maintained, Englishmen were in many cases actuated less by a desire for colonial emancipation than by a conviction that it was inevitable, a justified belief under the existing circumstances. Sometimes contemporaries did not mean to suggest complete and formal separation, but merely emancipation from the irksome control of the Colonial Office. Bodelsen also denounced later historians for showering unjustified opprobrium on critics of empire and advocates of separation. Few Englishmen of that day and age foresaw the emergence of something in the nature of a commonwealth of practically independent and equal nations. Partnership was not discussed; dependence or complete separation were generally considered to be the only possible alternatives.

Historians had also claimed that, by constant talk about the necessity or desirability of separation, Englishmen had wounded and exasperated colonial loyalty and thus actually brought nearer the disruption of the empire. Bodelsen pointed out, however, that the liberal policy of self-government and concession to colonial demands, to which the preservation of the empire could certainly be attributed, had in fact been greatly strengthened by the belief that the connection would be severed in the not too distant future. For several decades after the Canadian rebellions of 1837, the future of the empire had been precarious, and the strong tendencies towards separation in the colonies would probably have triumphed if the British government had attempted to arrest the process of devolution or to check the ambitions of the colonial legislatures. Such an attempt would undoubtedly have been made, Bodelsen argued, if statesmen with strong imperialist convictions had been in power in Britain at that crucial period. As it was, the British government remained passive or conciliatory, and in the colonies the knowledge that independence could always be secured for the asking made the few remaining imperial ties less galling. Paradoxically, therefore, the separatists and their ascendant influence over mid Victorian attitudes to colonies contributed positively to the continued unity of the empire.

ROBERT LIVINGSTON SCHUYLER:
THE FALL OF THE OLD COLONIAL SYSTEM *(1945)*

Because he had conducted a more comprehensive survey of British opinion than previous writers, Bodelsen argued that between 1830 and 1850 the Colonial Reformers constituted a small and unrepresentative group whose views on empire sharply contrasted with the prevailing scepticism and indifference of Englishmen. Moreover, their influence over British attitudes and policies was very shortlived and after 1850 gave way to a general separatist sentiment. A more extreme twist was given to this assessment in the writings of the American historian, Robert Livingston Schuyler (1883-1966), a professor of history at Columbia University. Schuyler described the first half of the nineteenth century as a period which saw the rise and triumph of anti-imperialist sentiment in Britain. His views were first set out in a series of articles which appeared in the *American Historical Review* and the *Political Science Quarterly* between 1917 and 1922. These articles were subsequently combined, with some new material, and published as a book, entitled *The Fall of the Old Colonial System, A Study in British Free Trade 1770-1870* (New York, 1945). This study was based principally on printed primary sources, such as *Hansard, Parliamentary Papers*, and contemporary books and pamphlets. Limited use was made of journals and newspapers, though such basic manuscript sources as the records of the Colonial Office and collections of private papers of leading figures were not consulted.

Schuyler's thesis was that the period from the American Revolution to 1870 saw the gradual rise of anti-imperialist sentiment in Britain, which reached its climax in the 1860's, and that this popular mood coincided with, and was related to, the downfall of the politico-economic system by which the first empire had been administered and the parallel growth of the movement for free trade. The fall of the old colonial system represented in Schuyler's view a major triumph for British liberalism in the history of the empire. If British statesmen had not outgrown the mentality of the colonial system, the emergence of the Commonwealth would have been impossible; independence could have come about only through successful rebellion against imperial authority, outside the structure of the empire. It would have been wholly contrary to the prevailing spirit of the traditional colonial system to allow colonies to attain autonomy within the empire or to permit them to withdraw peacefully.

Nevertheless, British liberals of all political persuasions were champions of indivdual liberty and free economic enterprise and rejected the old mercantilist conceptions of society, state, and empire. From the days of Adam Smith to those of Goldwin Smith, an increasing number of these liberals became avowed anti-imperialists, convinced that the disruption of the empire, by peaceful means if possible, would prove beneficial to the mother country, the colonies, and the world. Later writers in an imperialist age looked back on these mid Victorian liberals with amused contempt or reprobation as visionaries or crass materialists. Schuyler argued, however, that they were constructive critics of empire who made possible its evolution into a Commonwealth.

Since the rise of anti-imperialist sentiment in Britain was accompanied by the demise of the old colonial system and the growth of free-trade principles, Schuyler traced the origins of these developments to the attack on mercantilism launched by Adam Smith and other economists during and after the American Revolution. According to Schuyler, Smith "definitely associated anti-imperialism with *laissez-faire* economics, and the Manchester School looked back to him as the original Little-Englander". (p. 38) Consequently, a mounting attack on monopolies and commercial restrictions could be traced as the basis on which the old colonial system was undermined first by Smith and his contemporaries, then by the classical economists and Benthamites, and finally by the Manchester school. So long as the doctrines of mercantilism prevailed, colonies were prized because of the commercial benefits which the mother country derived from the monopoly of colonial trade, benefits which, it was believed, more than compensated for the burdens and responsibilities of empire. Contrary to mercantilist theory and contemporary expectations, however, the independence of the United States was followed, not by a marked decline in British exports and shipping, but by a substantial increase in Anglo-American trade. This development became a powerful argument for those who saw colonies as a source of weakness to Britain. Once commercial advantages no longer appeared to accrue from the restrictive regulation of imperial trade, Englishmen began to question the value of the empire. Furthermore, the American experience suggested that when colonies reached a degree of prosperity and maturity, they asserted their independence of the mother country. In this way, the fundamental tenets of mercantilism and the old colonial system were effectively challenged, and, as this attack was mounted, so British anti-imperialism began to emerge.

Although the criticisms levelled by Smith and others at the old colonial system in the late eighteenth century represented the "early English free-trade movement", Schuyler admitted that these utterances were neither representative of British opinion nor particularly influential at that time. The government did not immediately abandon its traditional commercial policies, adopt a more liberal form of colonial administration, or favour the independence of the remaining colonies. The emergence of a more general anti-imperialist sentiment was brought about by changes in the nature of the British economy, which converted a mercantile economy into an industrial economy, and by the movement for free trade which these changes generated. The mechanical inventions of the later eighteenth century gave British manufacturers such significant advantages over their foreign rivals that more reliance was placed on competitive superiority and less on legislative protection. With the growth of cheap, mass production, manufacturers became economic liberals and advocates of *laissez-faire*, and with these changed circumstances Adam Smith's ideas found a fertile soil.

Meanwhile, after the Napoleonic Wars, a group of political economists began to question the value of mercantilism and the colonial system. At a time when empire without commercial restriction seemed an anomaly, their teaching was naturally anti-imperialist in tone.

Closely related to the economists were the philosophical radicals, who recognized Jeremy Bentham as their leader. Schuyler maintained that in the writings of Mill, Ricardo, Malthus, and McCulloch, utilitarian philosophy and *laissez-faire* economics were all but fused. As free traders these men condemned the commercial restrictions of the colonial system as useless or pernicious since Britain could trade as profitably with foreign countries, as Britain's economic relations with the United States conclusively demonstrated. Furthermore, these illusory commercial benefits were accompanied by heavy burdens for the British taxpayer resulting from the expense of colonial government and defence. As radicals in politics, the economists and Benthamites denounced the bureaucratic, oppressive, and wastefully expensive system of colonial administration. Justice to the colonists and a concern for their true interests also demanded the abolition of the colonial system. British dominion over Canada was deleterious, the critics argued, both for the colonists and for Britain.

Schuyler, therefore, claimed that by the 1830's there had emerged in Britain a vocal and aggressive body of anti-imperialist opinion. The populace, as a whole, took no interest in the colonies, but amongst politicians and other public figures there was little enthusiasm for empire and little confidence that it would endure. To support this contention, Schuyler quoted the views of several political economists and Benthamites, as well as Lord Brougham in 1838, and Lord Melbourne in 1840. This odd assortment of opinions, cited without regard to the particular occasion and circumstances of their expression, hardly justifies the conclusion that vigorous anti-imperialism was developing in Britain in the thirties. Nevertheless, Schuyler believed that imperialists had now been put on the defensive; those who still avowed the usefulness of colonies felt obliged to justify their faith.

In Schuyler's discussion of British attitudes in the thirties and forties, little was said about the Colonial Reformers. The reason for this neglect is clear. The study was intentionally limited to colonial commerce and defence, and even in these fields no attempt was made to describe the administrative machinery which implemented imperial regulations and policies. Schuyler deliberately excluded the constitutional side of imperial relations from the scope of his inquiry, and he argued that the development of responsible government was too familiar to warrant detailed discussion. This was an entirely justifiable restriction in view of the nature of his study, but only so long as no claim was made that the represented views cited in the book fully reflected British opinion on colonies at that time. Yet this is what in fact occurs. On the basis of the views of free traders and a few critics of imperial defence and of the commercial restrictions of the old colonial system, Schuyler concluded that this was an age of growing anti-imperialism when Englishmen generally considered colonies politically, strategically, and economically valueless, and wished to be rid of them.

Due to his emphasis upon certain aspects of the time, a hiatus appeared in Schuyler's study when he discussed the 1830's. Schuyler alluded casually to a liberal imperialism that arose during the decade, of which Durham's *Report* was the most conspicuous landmark, but the point was not developed. The book falls into two distinct chronological parts: firstly, the rise of anti-imperialism coincident with the attacks of political economists on empire from Smith to Bentham and culminating in the commercial reforms of the 1820's; secondly, the triumph of anti- imperialism with the Manchester school, the coming of free trade, and the repeal of the Navigation Laws in the 1840's, leading to the climax of separatist sentiment in the sixties. In contrast, the thirties represented a quiet period in this drama, and are therefore ignored, except for the quotation of an occasional opinion by a British writer or statesman that seemed to prove the existence of universal indifference or scepticism towards colonies.

Once the views of writers and theorists had been discussed in some detail, the gradual collapse of the old colonial system could be traced through the modification and relaxation of commercial regulations during the sixty years or so after the loss of the American colonies, with particular reference to Huskisson's reforms in the 1820's and those of Peel's ministry between 1841 and 1846. Schuyler admitted that neither Huskisson nor Peel shared the prevailing pessimism regarding the empire or endorsed the doctrine of separatism. Huskisson's substitution of imperial preference and reciprocity for the old restrictive system was not designed to hasten the disruption of the empire. On the contrary, he regarded the introduction of a more liberal commercial policy as a means of effectively counteracting a colonial desire for separation. While Peel was deeply influenced by the free-trade ideas of the Manchester school, he was never a Little Englander. Nevertheless, Schuyler emphasized that these commercial reforms struck directly at the foundations of the imperial system and that many of those who supported the measures anticipated the dissolution of the empire as one of the beneficial results to be gained by the adoption of free trade.

The end of the old colonial system came with the repeal of the Navigation Laws in 1849. In the past, shipping had received special protection because of its contribution to British defence based on sea power, but the logic of free trade called for the abolition of protection for shipping as well as for agriculture and manufactures. In the course of the debate that preceded repeal, the colonial implications of the subject received much attention. Canadian opinion strongly favoured repeal and this fact was fully exploited by opponents of the laws in Britain. "Justice to the colonies" appeared an effective slogan, and free traders made the most of it, though their opponents were not slow to point out that colonial interests had been accorded little consideration in the earlier campaign against the corn laws. In actual fact, throughout the debate over the Navigation Laws the use of arguments relating to colonial welfare was largely dictated by expediency and the desire to reinforce the domestic implications of the issue.

Nevertheless, the advent of free trade, Schuyler concluded, could not fail to destroy the old British imperial system. Many of the apostles of the new commercial dispensation, accustomed as they were to identify the empire with the old colonial system, believed that the repudiation of the latter ultimately involved the dissolution of the former. Why should Britain, contemporaries asked themselves, continue to bear the burdens incident to the possession of colonies, when it derived from them no countervailing benefits? At the same time, the apparent tendency of colonies to separate from the mother country was often invested with the dignity of a natural law, and even some of those who were called colonial reformers regarded reform as a preliminary to emancipation. With free trade and responsible government also went a change in the system of colonial military defence and the withdrawal of imperial garrisons in the 1860's to ease the burdens of empire on the harassed British taxpayer. The recall of the imperial legions seemed to foretell the disintegration of the British empire.

But if the short-term effects of free trade came near to dissolving the empire, Schuyler pointed out that it also made possible in time a new concept of empire in which colonies were no longer dependencies but allies and partners, free to regulate their own affairs as they wished. Anti-imperialists contributed greatly to this transformation and the emergence of the Commonwealth, if not more than colonial reformers and liberal imperialists, certainly more than the late nineteenth century bombastic advocates of empire. Schuyler argued that this positive contribution had been neglected by historians who had shown nothing but contempt and abuse for the sceptics and critics of the mid Victorian empire. The revival of imperial sentiment in the late Victorian age, he felt, had "no doubt predisposed Englishmen, as historians, against dwelling upon what, as citizens, they would prefer to forget. Sometimes when an English historian does vouchsafe to touch upon the anti-imperial sentiment of the mid Victorian era the reader gets the impression that a regrettable episode is being glossed over." ("The Climax of Anti-Imperialism in England", *Political Science Quarterly*, XXXVI, 1921, p.539) The fact of the matter was that the anti-imperialists advocated, not the disintegration of the empire as such, but the abolition of the old colonial system, with its burdensome restrictions on the trade of the colonies and Britain, its subjection of the colonists to centralized bureaucratic control, and its vast expense to the British taxpayer. If working constitutional practice rather than legal forms was considered, Schuyler believed that the self-governing empire of his day conformed more nearly to the ideals of the mid Victorian anti-imperialists than to those of their opponents. It was they who made the Commonwealth possible by protecting the empire from its friends.

CONCLUSION

The writings of Bodelsen and Schuyler represent the most complete expression of a distinctive interpretation of British attitudes to empire in the second quarter of the nineteenth century. According to this view, that period formed an important stage in the gradual growth of anti-imperialist sentiment in Britain which reached its peak in the 1860's, a movement that was greatly accelerated and intensified by the coming of free trade and responsible government. In contrast to the widespread indifference of the general public and to the scepticism or pessimism of leading statesmen and writers, a small band of Colonial Reformers in the thirties and forties temporarily tried to revive the Englishman's confidence in the value and permanence of the empire but with limited and shortlived success.

This interpretation has exerted a considerable influence over historians, who have repeated these accepted views, most often uncritically, in a wide diversity of historical writings. There has thus grown up what can be regarded as the traditional explanation of British attitudes to empire in this period, an explanation that was particularly influential in the 1920's and 1930's, but which has continued to mesmerize historians down to the present day. While the following list is not intended to be exhaustive, the traditional interpretation is reflected in such articles as: D. G. Creighton, "The Victorians and the Empire", *Canadian Historical Review*, XIX, 1938, 138-53; Chester New, "Lord Durham and the British Background of his Report", *Canadian Historical Review*, XX, 1939, 119-35. Monographs that typically present this view include: Chester New, *Lord Durham* (Oxford, 1929); Chester Martin, *Empire and Commonwealth, Studies in Governance and Self-Government in Canada* (Oxford, 1929); C. P. Stacey, *Canada and the British Army 1846-1871: A Study in the Practice of Responsible Government* (London, 1936, and Toronto, 1968); Donald C. Gordon, *The Dominion Partnership in Imperial Defense, 1870-1914* (Baltimore, 1965). Amongst general histories of the British empire which offer the traditional interpretation can be mentioned: J. A. Williamson, *A Short History of British Expansion* (London, 1922); J. A. R. Marriott, *The Evolution of the British Empire and Commonwealth* (London, 1939); A. P. Newton, *A Hundred Years of the British Empire* (London, 1940); C. E. Carrington, *The British Overseas, Exploits of a Nation of Shopkeepers* (Cambridge, 1950); A. L. Burt, *The Evolution of the British Empire and Commonwealth* (New York, 1956).

PART 3

Towards a Revisionist Interpretation

Criticism of the views associated with the names of Bodelsen and Schuyler has been a gradual, unspectacular process. The first seeds of revision were sown by a few scholarly articles and monographs in the 1920's, at the same time that the traditional interpretation was being consolidated and accepted as the basis for general histories of British imperial activities in the nineteenth century. Since the 1950's, critical reappraisal has increasingly preoccupied the attention of specialists, though it has yet to produce a rewriting of the standard textbooks.

To some extent, changing conventions in imperial history have been encouraged by the exploitation of new sources of material. The examination of the official correspondence between secretaries of state and governors overseas, minutes, and memoranda contained in the Colonial Office papers at the Public Record Office in London has been particularly significant. This has given historians a deeper insight into the problems that confronted imperial administrators, into the way in which the empire was governed, and into the character and formation of policies. Recent writers have also made effective use of collections of private papers, which have often thrown new light on the personal opinions of leading contemporaries that were seldom expressed so frankly in public, and on the background behind official decisions and actions. Many contemporary myths and the speculations of those historians who did not have access to such official and private records have thereby been dispelled.

The reappraisal of accepted explanations, however, has been less the result of new material than of the more critical and thorough use of familiar sources. Historians have shown a greater awareness of the circumstances and context in which comments on the mid-Victorian empire were made, of the motives and prejudices of their authors, and of the audience to which the remarks were addressed. A conscious attempt has been made by several writers to appreciate contemporary opinion rather than apportion praise or blame. This more sophisticated, detached approach has been facilitated by the demise of popular imperialist sentiment in Britain and by the rise and decline of the Commonwealth. The mood of British opinion in the early and mid nineteenth century has thus been more carefully and appreciatively analysed. Sweeping generalizations have given way to an emphasis on the variety of shades of opinion and the frequent shifts in public attitudes. Greater subtlety and more searching inquiry have accordingly discouraged writers from dividing British opinion so rigorously into the categories of 'imperialist' and 'anti-imperialist'. Indeed, these and other generally accepted labels are now being discarded.

PAUL KNAPLUND:
STEPHEN, THE COLONIAL OFFICE,
AND GLADSTONE

The process of revision had its origins in the 1920's with the early writings of Paul Knaplund (1885-1964), an American historian who taught at the University of Wisconsin. A good example of the fruitful exploitation of new sources is provided by Knaplund's writings on James Stephen, the permanent under-secretary at the Colonial Office from 1836 to 1847, entitled: "Sir James Stephen and British North American Problems, 1840-1847", *Canadian Historical Review*, V, 1924, 22-41; "Mr. Oversecretary Stephen", *Journal of Modern History*, I, 1929, 40-66; *James Stephen and the British Colonial System 1813-1847* (Madison, 1953). Contemporaries believed that effective power within the colonial department rested in Stephen's hands, and that since he opposed all measures of reform, he personified the irresponsible, bureaucratic despotism under which the colonists groaned. These accusations were generally unsubstantiated, but the criticisms voiced by Buller, Wakefield, and other critics of colonial administration were zealously propagated and widely quoted. Later it became customary for historians to accept these biased conjectures as authentic evidence. Knaplund's study of the Colonial Office correspondence and Stephen's minutes and memoranda clearly revealed, however, that his traducers grossly exaggerated the power and effectiveness of the colonial department as an agency for governing a scattered empire, and overestimated the degree of Stephen's influence over the formation of imperial policy. Moreover, he actively encouraged the spirit of reform; at a relatively early date he was prepared to endow the Canadians with a large measure of local autonomy, and he tried unsuccessfully to revitalize the cumbersome administrative machinery in Whitehall for governing the empire.

Knaplund's critical reassessment of accepted explanations was also pursued in his examination of William Gladstone's opinions on empire in "Gladstone's Views on British Colonial Policy", *Canadian Historical Review*, IV, 1923, 304-15, and *Gladstone and Britain's Imperial Policy* (London, 1927). These studies were designed to show how a leading statesman's attitudes to the empire changed during the course of the nineteenth century. Gladstone initially entertained conservative views about the incompatibility of colonial self-government and imperial supremacy and expressed considerable scepticism over the preservation of the empire. But as a result of ministerial experience during the 1840's, he was converted to a more liberal, optimistic point of view, and he came to see kindred sentiment and mutual interest as the basis of a continuing relationship. Knaplund defended Gladstone against the earlier writers' charge of 'anti-imperialism'. Not only was the liberalism of the mid nineteenth century which conceded colonial self-government constructive statesmanship of the highest order, but Gladstone's views were too subtle and varied to be labelled as either 'imperialist' or 'anti-imperialist'.

KLAUS E. KNORR:
BRITISH COLONIAL THEORIES 1570-1850 *(1944)*

While revision of the Bodelsen-Schuyler thesis has been a piecemeal process, one relatively comprehensive examination of British attitudes to empire was provided by Klaus E. Knorr in *British Colonial Theories 1570-1850* (Toronto, 1944). This book represented an ambitious attempt to survey British theories about colonies from Elizabethan to mid Victorian times. It was based on an impressive canvass of material in the form of books, pamphlets, parliamentary debates, some periodicals, and some published papers of statesmen, though newspapers and primary manuscript sources such as private papers and Colonial Office records were not consulted. Throughout his discussion, Knorr showed a clearer understanding of the nature of colonial policy and its relationship with public opinion than many earlier writers. He demonstrated how the "development of colonial theories influenced motives that produced action and significantly fashioned the formulation of policies" (p. xvii), and how British political and economic changes affected attitudes to empire and official policies. Unfortunately, Knorr failed to consider the impact of colonial developments and conditions on the course of imperial policy or British attitudes. Not only was the topic approached very much from the British point of view, but theories and policies were discussed without sufficient reference to the actual course of events and imperial practice throughout the empire.

Although Knorr covered fairly familiar ground in the period 1815-50, the diverse facets and themes of imperial activity examined in the book offered a wide sampling of opinions and did not suggest that one group reflected the dominant attitude in any given period. Moreover, he did not attempt to divide contemporary opinion into imperialist and anti-imperialist, but, on the contrary, discerned nuances and changes in the views of individuals and groups. This more discriminating approach was apparent in a discussion of the classical economists and empire, with particular reference to the writings of Bentham, James Mill, and Ricardo. Their views were examined in more detail than previous imperial historians had attempted and more weight was given to their favourable comments on empire. While Bentham and Mill denounced the inutility of colonies and the evils of the colonial system, they did not clearly state whether or not Britain should relinquish its existing possessions. They felt that Britain had a responsibility to make overseas settlements free and prosperous, and for Britain to abandon the colonies precipitately might be to sacrifice the welfare of their inhabitants. Moreover, the empire offered a vast field for experiments in philanthropy and reform which could not be practised at home. Such a concept of empire, Knorr argued, was almost identical to that later entertained by the liberal opponents of separatism, such as Earl Grey, who advanced arguments to justify the maintenance of the empire in terms very similar to those employed by the Benthamites. Furthermore, many economists were reluctant to advocate the abandonment of colonies because they were gravely concerned about the signs of overpopulation in Britain. The possibility that colonization might relieve domestic difficulties made the retention and even the extension of the empire palatable to many economists and statesmen who would otherwise have been inclined to regard colonies with indifference or disfavour. To some extent, Bentham and James Mill shared in this conversion, and when Wakefield put forward his idea of systematic colonization, the majority of the Benthamites, especially Molesworth,

J. S. Mill, and George Grote, became ardent advocates of the new movement.

Knorr then proceeded to examine attitudes to emigration and colonization. Although he had little new to say on the topic, his discussion was comprehensive. He divided the principal currents of thought on these subjects into two chronological periods. From 1815 to the early 1830's the main consideration was the removal of paupers and labourers to alleviate the widespread unemployment and the heavy burden of poor relief. From the early thirties to 1850, however, the prevailing topic of public discussion was systematic colonization, which was designed to relieve distress amongst all classes of British society, to provide additional outlets for the profitable investment of surplus British capital, and to create new producing areas and markets overseas. Wakefield was the foremost advocate of this movement, though the principles of his theory were of less importance in the history of British imperial thought than the Wakefieldians' incessant and effective propaganda for the cause of colonization as such. Knorr also emphasized the concern of the Wakefieldians and other contemporaries for the multiplication of little Englands overseas. They considered it desirable to provide the emigrant with a familiar social environment in the colonies, and to transplant overseas British political institutions, customs, and civilization through the migration of all ranks of English society. The colonists would thus be less responsive to extreme democratic ideas, and a strong and lasting link would be created between mother country and daughter colonies. English writers of the day often compared British colonization with that of the ancient Greeks. This belief in the cultural mission of British colonizing activity gained wide currency.

When Knorr examined the contemporary debate over the merits and methods of emigration, he pointed out that Englishmen spoke without experience and had to rely on theoretical assumptions and conclusions. While there was general agreement on the basic nature of Britain's plight, opinion differed concerning the efficacy of emigration as a remedy, the methods of financing large-scale migration, and the desirable degree of state activity. Some Englishmen criticized extensive emigration on the grounds that it deprived Britain of useful population, was expensive to subsidize, and entailed an injurious outflow of capital. Wilmot Horton sought to convince the critics that it would be cheaper to send paupers overseas than maintain them in idleness at home, and that loans from government or parishes might be repaid by the emigrants. But the questions of expense and capital drain assumed an entirely different complexion once Wakefield revolutionized the whole matter by placing emigration on a self-supporting basis and showing how the diminution of the country's surplus capital would be economically advantageous. As for the role of the state, few people advocated compulsory emigration, and at the other extreme only the most uncompromising disciples of *laissez-faire* disapproved of all forms of state action in the case of voluntary emigration. Government assistance might take many forms and degrees of intervention, but generally politicians were reluctant to sanction more than a minimum amount of official support. Emigration to North America proceeded unsubsidized and largely unsupervised, and the government did nothing to encourage the flow of migrants towards Canada rather than the United States, which the unaided majority apparently preferred.

Knorr then turned his attention to the fall of the old colonial system with a brief reference to Huskisson's reforms in the 1820's and a more detailed examination of the subsequent debate over the sugar and timber duties. While advocates of free trade concentrated their attack against the corn laws, next in importance were the duties on sugar and timber, both of which involved a consideration of imperial preference and of the whole colonial system. The prolonged debate over the Canadian timber duties illustrated contemporary views on the value of the North American provinces, though the attitudes toward colonies of participants in the debate were largely determined by their support for or opposition to the principle of protection. Argument centred around the relationship between imperial preference for Canadian timber and the contribution to British naval superiority of shipping engaged in the timber trade, and around the question whether this shipping represented a nursery of naval power or simply a means of transportation. There was also discussion on whether the state should protect British shipping and Canadian timber interests, even if preferential duties encouraged the import of expensive and inferior timber. Critics argued that particular interests should not be supported at the expense of the consumer and the community at large, and that the existing duties encouraged uneconomic investment of capital on the part of the Canadians. Discussion also turned on the relative importance and security of colonies and foreign countries as sources of raw materials and as markets for British goods. Free traders placed reliance on the cheapness of British exports and general commercial predominance, while protectionists feared foreign competition and advocated imperial self-sufficiency and the dependability of colonial markets and sources of supply. Knorr pointed out, however, that not all free traders were hostile to colonial possessions. The Wakefieldians championed free trade but perceived distinct advantages from the preservation and extension of the empire. Earl Grey and others optimistically assumed that colonies would adhere to the free trade policy of Britain and remain good customers even in the absence of tariff preferences because of a similarity of origins, institutions, customs, and tastes.

The abolition of imperial preferences and the Navigation Laws was bound to follow the repeal of the corn laws in 1846, because the principle of free trade could be as logically applied to other colonial products and navigation as to corn. In the case of the Navigation Laws, British shipowners and shipbuilders were able to protract the debate, because they enjoyed the support of other groups interested in the maintenance of protection, and because of the widespread conviction that there was a close connection between the protection of British shipping and the strength of British seapower. Traditional mercantilist notions continued to be widely held at least until the 1840's, and while free traders drew heavily on arguments supplied by the classical economists, the progress of economic theory had only a very gradual influence on British commercial policy and the downfall of the old colonial system.

Knorr suggested that British attitudes to empire during these years could not be fully appreciated without reference to certain additional items in what he called "the balance-sheet of imperialism". One important issue concerned the cost of governing and defending the empire at the expense of the British taxpayer. Throughout the period, radicals and liberals persistently condemned this onerous burden, though their opponents branded them as narrow-minded economizers who reduced everything to a matter of pounds, shillings, and pence. In order to ease this financial burden, some Englishmen suggested emancipating the colonies, but the vast majority proposed a more or less drastic reduction in current expenditure. Since most proposals meant that the colonists would shoulder a larger portion of their civil and military expenses, the implementation of demands for economy necessitated the concession of greater colonial self-government. The expense of the North American provinces to the British taxpayer was therefore substantially diminished once the colonies were well on the way to becoming dominions, and the movement towards local autonomy was sustained by the demands of the economy-minded faction in Britain, as well as by the constitutional programme of the metropolitan liberals and the aspirations of the colonists themselves.

The more intangible factors that influenced British opinion also had to be taken into consideration. Various arguments were advanced to suggest that colonies augmented the military power of Britain, and politicians often emphasized the prestige that the possession of a large colonial empire bestowed on the parent state. Although spokesmen of the Manchester school might ridicule these arguments, Knorr maintained that pride of empire constituted an extremely powerful sentiment in favour of the retention and even the expansion of overseas possessions. Many Englishmen thought that Britain was destined by providence to perform the lofty mission of spreading peace, order, and civilization throughout the world, a responsibility which had to be shouldered even if it involved material sacrifices. Knorr admitted that contemporary panegyrics on the expansion of Anglo-Saxon civilization and the unselfish duty owed to colonists in particular and mankind in general might often have been rationalizations of baser, materialistic, and even discreditable motives. But he felt that it would be erroneous to question the sincerity of everyone who subscribed to these emotional and psychological arguments, and certainly references to Britain's mission steadily increased in number and frequency as the nineteenth century progressed.

When Knorr made some general comments on British opinion during these years, he emphasized the close relationship that existed between alterations in Britain's commercial policy and changing attitudes to colonies. With this point in mind, he examined the views of politicians concerning the empire. Though Whigs and Tories comprised motley coalitions, it could generally be said that the majority of Tories supported protectionism, while the bulk of the Whigs took up the cause of free trade. Yet it could not be argued that the Whigs were less concerned about the preservation of the empire than the Tories; they were merely less interested in maintaining the traditional colonial policies and practices with which the Tories identified themselves. The approach of the two parties to colonial questions reflected a different conception of empire. More members of the Whig than the Tory party regarded the ultimate emancipation of the colonies as inevitable, and they were unwilling to keep adult communities within the empire by compulsory methods. It was particularly this latter consideration which led Whig ministers to replace preferential commercial regulations with sentimental attachments as the cement of empire and made them more willing than the Tories to extend the principle of colonial self-government.

Knorr maintained that until about 1830, the radicals in politics tended to regard the empire as a heavy burden, though their hostility was directed against the old colonial system rather than against the empire as such. With the rise of the Wakefield school in the 1830's, however, the majority of the radicals joined forces with the Colonial Reformers. They formed a small but energetic and vociferous group with an ardent faith in the future of a self-governing empire. With their advocacy of further colonization, theirs was an expansionist imperialism, yet most of them were also free traders and critics of colonial expenditure. Nevertheless, Knorr made the important point that the distinctiveness and unity of the Colonial Reformers could easily be exaggerated. This lack of agreement could be seen in their reaction to the Canadian rebellions and Lord Durham's mission. Amongst the various radical groups, the greatest consistency could be found in the attitude of the Manchester school. They wanted to relieve Britain from the burdens of empire, even if this process resulted in the empire's dissolution, though they would not have been opposed on principle to a commonwealth free from protectionist regulations and without expense to British taxpayers.

In his discussion of British attitudes to empire, Knorr did not characterize the period as one of anti-imperialism, nor did he contrast the views of the Colonial Reformers with a prevailing scepticism. On the contrary, he concluded that the views of Englishmen about the empire contained many similarities. It had to be admitted that there was considerable apathy and ignorance amongst the British public. The politicians and writers actively interested in colonial questions constituted only a very small minority of the British people, and even amongst the governing and thinking classes, indifference was more widespread a phenomenon than separatism. While Englishmen might criticize and complain about misgovernment and expense, very few voices unequivocally demanded the abandonment of the colonies. Advocacy of separation was confined to a small group of Little Englanders, composed mainly of the leaders of the Manchester school, some economists, and radicals like Hume. Yet even Cobdenites and Little Englanders, Knorr argued, would have found nothing objectionable in an empire thrown open to the free flow of world trade and composed of self-governing communities, paying for their own administration and defence, and enjoying independence in everything but name. "To the vast majority of Little Englanders, Little Englandism and a liberal British Commonwealth of Nations were absolutely compatible objectives." (p. 375) In other words, very little difference could be discerned in the attitudes to empire of the Manchester school, of liberals like Russell, Grey, and Gladstone, and of such Colonial Reformers as Wakefield and Molesworth.

Moreover, the fundamental issue in the contemporary debate was colonial reform, not the question of separation versus the preservation of the empire. Critics of the colonial system and its evils did not intend the empire to be disrupted by their campaign. The demand for the abolition of tariff preferences and British expenditure on colonial government and defence was a demand for separation only if the existing imperial system should prove incapable of being reformed along these lines. Britain's adoption of free trade and colonial self-government did not represent conscious or unconscious 'decolonization' as many Tory contemporaries and some later writers alleged.

Far from describing the period 1815-50 as one of anti-imperialism, Knorr concluded that separatism and indifference were surprisingly uninfluential. Not only were the advocates of a Little England policy extremely few in number, but they had to fight against very heavy odds, since the popular sentiment of most classes favoured the retention of colonies. While the British people took the symbols of empire for granted, the loss of any major part of it would certainly have been regarded as a humiliating shock to national pride and power. In addition to certain British interests which had a commercial or financial stake in the various dependencies, Englishmen had acquired what Knorr called the habit of empire; they were accustomed to think in terms of empire and to perform the role of an imperial power without inquiring into the utility of doing so. It also had to be admitted that the colonists themselves, for sentimental or other reasons, did not want to separate from the empire once they were able to do so.

As tangible evidence of the limited influence of separatist sentiment, Knorr alluded briefly to the substantial territorial expansion of the British empire during these years. He considered the acquisition of vast territories in Australasia, India, and Africa an astonishing phenomenon in view of the current of indifference and hostility to colonies in Britain. This expansion was the product of many forces unrelated to British opinion: unchallenged command of the sea, the absence of foreign rivalry, and the extension of existing frontiers by the action of officials and traders on the spot or by other local exigencies. Imperial expansion between 1815 and 1850 was not the outcome of a determined policy of extending the frontiers of the empire. Nevertheless, Knorr believed that the lack of resolute resistance in London to such expansion could be explained only by the fact that the attitudes of scepticism and separatism, however vociferously expressed, were on the whole weaker than the forces which counteracted their influence. A policy of imperial withdrawal or the abandonment of the colonies was never seriously envisaged by any responsible British statesman, and popular sentiment would probably have been opposed to such a course of action. Knorr's comments here only cursorily touched upon the vital question of the relationship between British attitudes and the actual development of the empire, but he said enough to indicate the unreality of discussing public opinion on colonial questions without fully relating it to imperial practice and the actual course of events. Unless this broader factual context is used as the framework of imperial history, a study of British attitudes and colonial theories becomes a meaningless academic exercise.

HELEN TAFT MANNING:
IMPERIAL POLICY AND ATTITUDES
TO BRITISH NORTH AMERICA

Since the publication of Knorr's book in 1944, there has been no comprehensive examination of British attitudes to empire during the years 1822-1849, and further consideration of the matter has been given only in a limited and often indirect fashion in articles and monographs that have been concerned with some small aspect of the topic or with marginally related themes. Some writers, for example, have provided a reappraisal of the personnel, administrative practices, and policies of the Colonial Office, and this has incidentally elucidated the attitudes of officials and politicians. Others have considered the interrelationship amongst public opinion, imperial policies, and developments overseas, generally illustrated with reference to the late Victorian empire. Consequently, the concluding part of this historiographical survey deals largely with writings on small facets of the topic under consideration or with work in associated fields that has some particular relevance or implications for the subject.

In the course of her inquiries into the nature of colonial administration and imperial relations during these years, Helen Taft Manning has made a major contribution towards a better understanding of English policies and attitudes towards British North America. The most important studies for the present discussion include: "The Colonial Policy of the Whig Ministers, 1830-37", *Canadian Historical Review*,

XXXIII, September and December 1952, 203-36, 341-68; "Colonial Crises Before the Cabinet, 1828-1835", *Bulletin of the Institute of Historical Research*, XXX, 1957, 41-61; *The Revolt of French Canada 1800-1835, A Chapter in the History of the British Commonwealth* (Toronto, 1962); "Who Ran the British Empire—1830-1850?", *Journal of British Studies*, V, 1965, 88-121.

Historians had fostered the legend that ignorance and indifference were the leading characteristics of British opinion on matters connected with British North America and the empire at least before 1837, if not thereafter. This indictment, Manning maintained, showed a complete misconception of British attitudes. There were, of course, radicals in parliament who denounced the colonies as valueless, but responsible statesmen were profoundly concerned about such matters as the territorial ambitions and the commercial, maritime rivalry of the United States. They were anxious to avoid another colonial catastrophe in North America and they feared the outbreak of war with the American republic. With the memory of American victories during the War of 1812 still firmly implanted in their minds, ministers were prepared to devote large sums of the British taxpayers' money to building up the defence of the Canadas at a time when the parliamentary radicals were demanding retrenchment. Though British possessions in North America were vulnerable to attack, they did at least help to check the further expansion of the United States. Although few Englishmen believed that Canada would ever become commercially valuable as a colony, possession of Canada would enable Britain to conduct a possible war with the neighbouring republic. Such a war would be expensive and unprofitable, but in view of what Englishmen considered the erratic course of American democracy, especially on the frontier, it was an eventuality which ministers did not ignore, and they prepared for it as best they could. The expedient of abandoning the North American colonies to the United States was a course of action which at that time had no appeal for leading English statesmen.

Manning also emphasized that the imagination of politicians and businessmen was increasingly captured by the possibility of exploiting the undeveloped resources of North America. The City of London showed particular interest in the investment of capital in British colonies, especially after disillusionment with South America had followed the panic of 1825. While the United States remained the most promising field for both investment and emigration, there was growing apprehension in Britain that the republic was becoming a dangerous rival in foreign trade and shipbuilding. In these circumstances, the development of Canada's natural resources offered a means of meeting the American challenge and benefiting British capitalists and merchants. The progress of the timber trade and the shipbuilding industries of New Brunswick and the St. Lawrence region suggested that other parts of the continent might be profitably exploited. As Huskisson and others argued, commerce and investment were the most effective guarantees Britain could find against American ambitions.

At the same time, the expansion of British settlement would foster Canadian development. When emigration came to be accepted by the 1820's as an appropriate means of relieving the economic and social problems of the mother country, Canada grew in importance as an outlet for Britain's 'surplus' population. Although public opinion and imperial policy on the subject of emigration were still undecided in the twenties, statistics showed that Canada had already become the most attractive country within the empire for British migrants. The activities and propaganda of the Wakefieldians after 1830 made the public even more fully aware of the steady stream of emigration to North America. Canada thus assumed a new imperial significance, and one that had a direct bearing on the political controversy of the period. With their demands for control over the whole valley of the lower St. Lawrence, the French Canadians came to be regarded by Englishmen as an obstacle to economic progress and British ambitions. However loyal the French inhabitants might be to the British crown, their outlook and designs appeared inimical to the interests of the British merchants who were busily developing the commercial possibilities of the St. Lawrence region as the gateway to the interior of the North American continent and to future British settlement in the area.

In her reassessment of British opinion and imperial administration during these years, Professor Manning also examined the role of parliament in colonial affairs and the attitudes of members of the House of Commons to imperial and Canadian questions. For many years after the loss of the American colonies, she pointed out, British politicians tacitly agreed that parliament should not again become involved in the administration of the colonial empire. From the passage of the Canadian Constitutional Act of 1791, until the act emancipating the slaves within the empire was carried in 1833, no significant measure relating to the internal affairs of the colonies was approved by the House of Commons. This long abstinence was not so much the result of indifference to colonial affairs amongst members of the Commons, as some writers had suggested, but reflected a determination that parliament should not again become embroiled in conflict with a colonial legislature. Parliamentary authority should be held in reserve and employed as an impartial endorsement of agreements reached by the British government with the colonists, and should not be used to impose on the Canadians or other peoples a constitutional formula devised in London. Many members of parliament, for example, both Whig and Tory, were opposed to any amendment of the Act of 1791 unless convincing evidence was provided that alterations were needed, and some argued that such a step would violate promises given by the British government to the French Canadians in 1774. Moreover, successive ministries preferred whenever possible to exclude colonial affairs from parliament and tackle them as administrative rather than as legislative questions. But while ministers could normally prevent controversial colonial measures from being introduced, they could not check mounting criticism of imperial administration which developed, especially between 1827 and 1830, and thereafter remained a factor of intermittent significance in the political world.

Clearer than any previous writer Manning demonstrated the way in which colonial issues had parliamentary repercussions, especially after 1827, with the signs of growing political discontent in the Canadas and the West Indies and mounting criticism in the House of Commons of the inept and illiberal colonial policy of the ministry of the day. The Tory administrations of the late 1820's were assailed by radicals and Whigs who denounced the expense, and sometimes the uselessness, of colonies. A particularly vocal group of radicals, led by Joseph Hume, persistently criticized the substantial sums of money being spent on the government and defence of the empire, and with British North America principally in mind, argued that colonies should either be emancipated or made responsible for their own administration. In their demands for retrenchment, the radicals maintained that if the colonists were free to manage their own affairs, they would then assume the whole expense of their civil governments and military establishments. Allegations of extravagance and accusations of tyranny in colonial administration therefore provided excellent political pretexts in the late twenties for the parliamentary opposition to attack the Tory ministry of the day. From this time onwards, colonial problems assumed a new importance in British politics and cabinets were forced to turn their attention to an unfamiliar area of ministerial activity. The concern for colonial questions persisted after 1830 when the Whigs came into office, though the major ground for assailing government policies tended to shift from the issue of economy to that of bureaucracy. This transition occurred when the Colonial Reformers replaced the parliamentary radicals as the chief critics of Colonial Office and ministry, and when the problems involved in the government of Canada came to preoccupy the attention of the House of Commons.

As Manning clearly showed, British North America, and particularly Lower Canada, provided parliamentary critics during these years with excellent ammunition to support their accusations. From the time of the assembly's appeal against the authoritarian administration of Governor Dalhousie in 1828, the potential supporters of Lower Canada in the British House of Commons were numerous and for the moment formidable. There was considerable sympathy for the French Canadian cause in 1828, and the report of the select committee on the civil government of Canada would not have been so favourable to the assembly of Lower Canada but for the general feeling amongst members of parliament that the Act of 1791 could not be lightly set aside. Nevertheless, the French Canadians soon lost much of this support. The reformed parliament was preoccupied with domestic legislation, and amongst colonial matters, the abolition of slavery appeared more urgent than the settlement of the affairs of Lower Canada. When the radicals once more took up the cause of the Canadas in 1834, events had proceeded too rapidly for particular constitutional grievances to be effectively presented in the Commons. Furthermore, the assembly's demands had grown more extreme by 1834 and the sympathies of most members of parliament had been alienated by the colonists' rejection of conciliatory overtures from London. Roebuck, as agent for the assembly, kept the Canadian problem before the Commons with the assistance of philosophic radicals like Molesworth, but by 1834 the protection of British interests in North America and those of the English settlers in Lower Canada secured greater parliamentary support than the seemingly republican and revolutionary proposals of the French Canadians.

Another of Manning's major contributions has been an examination of the attitudes of the Whigs as evidenced by their policy over the Canadian question in the 1830's. According to the traditional explanation, British policy towards the North American provinces remained both illiberal and basically unchanged until it was rudely shattered by the unexpected Canadian rebellions in 1837 and subsequently reconstructed by Lord Durham and the Colonial Reformers. Such an interpretation of imperial relations, Manning maintained, made insufficient allowance for the mood of reform in Britain after 1830 and the enlightened, conscientious efforts of the Whigs to resolve an intractable problem. Even though few Englishmen had a personal acquaintance with the colonies, and measures designed to meet changing conditions depended greatly on improvisation and *a priori* reasoning and were often ineptly implemented, the Whigs' approach to Canadian questions was far from reactionary and unsympathetic. As a party, they were firmly committed to the pursuit of economy in the government of colonies. Parliamentary demands for retrenchment found a positive response with Lord Howick's advent at the Colonial Office in 1830, as he energetically tried to reduce the current expenditure on colonial civil, military, and ecclesiastical establishments. Although efforts to transfer financial responsibilities to the colonists often created friction, the Whigs endorsed the view that economy for Britain and redress of colonial grievances went hand in hand, and this reasoning was unquestionably sound from the long-range point of view. Whig ministries were also prepared to concede to the inhabitants of British North America control over their own internal affairs and extend to them through appropriate reforms the full benefits of the British constitution. Imperial policy towards Canada after 1830 was therefore overtly based on the principle of conciliation.

Despite a relatively liberal philosophy of colonial government and a sincere desire to bring about greater harmony in Anglo-Canadian relations, most of the Whigs' attempts at reform were thwarted by the inability in any colony of governors, councils, and assemblies to reach agreement on the precise form of self-government they wanted. The British government refused to impose a settlement in these circumstances because it wanted to preserve the loyalty of the inhabitants and because it was deeply committed to the non-intervention of the imperial parliament in colonial affairs. Moreover, the attention given by ministers to the political problems of British North America was preoccupied with the developing crisis in Lower Canada. And here the proposals of the extremist French Canadian leaders, as embodied in the famous resolutions of 1834, represented demands which no Whig politician, however anxious to conciliate, would entertain. Gradual changes in the legal codes and administration of the provincial governments were acceptable, but ministers preferred not to become involved in uncertain constitutional experiments that savoured of democracy and insidious American influences; popular conventions, elective councils, and other radical revisions of the structure of colonial government were anathema to statesmen whose outlook on such matters was fashioned by a reverence for the hallowed British constitution. Few politicians in the thirties were prepared to support demands for an elective legislative council, especially when circumstances in Lower Canada would have produced an unacceptable French majority, and the concept of a responsible colonial executive in Canada was considered inconsistent with colonial status. Nevertheless, Manning argued that the Whigs in the 1830's were in fact moving in the general direction of cabinet government for Canada after the British model, whether or not they were fully conscious of the fact. Indeed, ministers could not have proceeded much further or faster in the direction of responsible government at this particular time, without giving colonial assemblies more power than was claimed by the House of Commons, and in the event the final steps had to be taken by governors acting as the crown's representatives. To have determined that councillors be regularly chosen to meet the wishes of the majority of the assembly would have been incompatible with the current conventions of the British constitution. Constitutional objections to conferring responsible government before the mid-forties were thus as serious as practical objections.

The fact that the British government failed to find an immediate solution to the Canadian crisis in the 1830's did not reflect the indifference or illiberality of ministers. Failure had to be attributed to the intractable nature of the problems confronting them, particularly in view of the lack of accurate information in London about political conditions in the colonies, the deficiencies of the colonial civil service, and the frequent cabinet changes in Britain. Meanwhile the discussion of Canadian questions turned on fundamental issues and the outlook of ministers suggested a deeper understanding of conditions overseas than did the views of radicals like Roebuck and Hume, who urged concessions to particular Canadian factions without appreciating the predicament in which this would have placed the rest of the colonists. Whig ministers tried to balance the interests of all sections of the colonial communities, and in their attempts to translate generous sympathies into an acceptable settlement of colonial grievances, Manning maintained that they showed a degree of liberality and responsibility for which historians had not given them sufficient credit.

GALLAGHER AND ROBINSON, MACDONAGH, AND GRAMPP: FREE TRADE—IMPERIALISM OR ANTI-IMPERIALISM?

While Manning's study of British policy towards Canada in the 1830's has suggested the need for some modification of the traditional view of English attitudes to empire, other writers have thrown light on this question by examining the relationship between British opinion and the course of imperial development. Recent investigation of this theme was begun in a celebrated article by John Gallagher and Ronald Robinson, "The Imperialism of Free Trade", *Economic History Review*, VI, 1953, 1-15. They criticized the traditional description of imperial sentiment and activity in the early and mid-Victorian period as 'anti-imperialist' in character and questioned the accepted belief that statesmen and officials of that day were hostile towards expansionism and indifferent even to the preservation of the existing empire. These false assumptions originated with historians who had focused their attention too exclusively on Canada and the other settlement colonies, or what might be called the 'formal' empire, in contrast to the 'informal' empire of territories dominated by British investment and trading activities. The orthodox view of imperial history in the nineteenth century remained that expounded by such writers as Seeley and Egerton, who entertained a political and legalistic concept of empire, and who considered events in the area of formal dominion as the sole evidence of imperial activity. The century was thus divided into periods of early and mid Victorian 'anti-imperialism' and late Victorian 'imperialism' according to the contraction or expansion of the formal empire and the extent to which Englishmen appeared to value British rule over these territories. At the same time, the authors suggested that historians had drawn too direct and facile a connection between the prevailing scepticism or enthusiasm for empire and the rise and decline of the belief in free trade.

A similar discrepancy could be seen in the matter of imperial constitutional policy. If responsible government was granted to Canada and other colonies as a result of mid Victorian apathy or hostility to empire, there seemed no reason why the policy was continued in the late Victorian period when Britain was concerned above all to preserve imperial unity. But in fact, the authors argued, throughout the century responsible government was conceded only where it would not endanger British interests or paramountcy. In areas where statesmen feared a foreign challenge to British supremacy, or a colony was unable to meet the cost of its own security, the imperial authorities retained full responsibility. The concession of responsible government was not therefore a means of hastening the disruption of the empire, but evidence of a shift from direct to indirect methods of upholding British interests. If formal political ties could be safely loosened, it was then possible to rely on economic dependence and mutual goodwill to bind colonies to the mother country. Supremacy in Canada could accordingly be surrendered in the forties and fifties without endangering vital British concerns; indeed contemporaries saw this surrender as a means of strengthening them.

In order to explain the apparent contradictions in attitudes and policies, Gallagher and Robinson emphasized the basic continuity of imperial development in the nineteenth century and the need to consider both informal and formal methods of expansion. Governments were willing at all times to ensure the security of British trade and investment by active intervention, but the means of establishing and maintaining British paramountcy varied according to the circumstances of the diverse regions of imperial interest. At any given period different territories had reached different stages of economic exploitation and integration into the British economy; thus varying degrees of political control were required to secure the maximum economic opportunities. Nevertheless, informal methods were preferred whenever possible, and formal methods were employed only when necessary. This preference for informal means largely explained the differing character of mid and late Victorian imperial development. Informal techniques were more often adequate in the circumstances of the mid century than in the later period when foreign rivalries developed. But extension of direct British rule and expensive involvement remained a last resort at all times, and this reluctance gave rise to the many 'anti-expansionist' remarks made by British ministers. Historians had seized on these and, with other seemingly critical or sceptical comments of the period, had described a prevailing mood of early and mid Victorian anti-imperialism. What these contemporary comments obscured, and later writers ignored, was that in practice administrators and statesmen were prepared to protect British interests by the extension of formal rule whenever informal methods failed to provide adequate security. The concept of 'the age of anti-imperialism' was an inaccurate description of both British attitudes and overseas activities during these years.

While Gallagher and Robinson did not specifically relate their arguments to British North America, their article is significant to the present discussion because it criticized certain enduring deficiencies in writings on imperial history in the nineteenth century, and because it began a continuing debate on the nature of British imperialism in that period and on the relationship between overseas enterprise and free trade. The ramifications of this debate go beyond the scope of this survey, but a couple of points at issue have some relevance. Amongst the many critical comments on the earlier article was the rejoinder by Oliver MacDonagh in "The Anti-Imperialism of Free Trade", *Economic History Review*, XIV, 1962, 489-501. MacDonagh admitted that the essentially imperialist character of British policy and of much public sentiment in the forties and fifties had now been validly established, and that the contrary myth long advanced by historians had accordingly been effectively dispelled. Nevertheless, the thesis argued by Gallagher and Robinson had ignored the fact that mid Victorian imperialist sentiment and activity was persistently, and sometimes successfully, challenged. It was particularly misleading in this respect to suggest that free traders promoted the growth of the empire, when in fact they condemned many aspects of imperial expansion as a crime against the true principles of free trade. Historians had made the mistake, MacDonagh maintained, of describing both the Manchester school and the Whigs after 1846 as free traders. This oversimplification obscured the inveterate hostility of the Manchester radicals to such matters as aristocratic government, unnecessary state activity, avoidable public expenditure, the armed services, and aggressive imperialism. They denounced the opening up of overseas markets by force, because they regarded free trade as essentially pacific and 'natural' in growth, and they criticized an empire which supported an aristocratic caste that promoted wars and hatreds, and led to the squandering of resources. Although MacDonagh regarded the Manchester free traders as anti-imperialists, he admitted that they lacked political power and failed to influence the leading politicians in imperial affairs. Moreover, the views of Cobden and others were out of tune with the prevailing sentiments of the British electorate after 1846 with its support for aggressive Palmerstonian diplomacy, if not for imperial expansion.

But MacDonagh argued that it was important not to neglect the existence of opposition to imperialism, and thus to deny variety to British opinion and imperial policy in the Victorian age. Indeed, he believed that the forces of imperialism and anti-imperialism were engaged in an unending if intermittent struggle, with fluctuating fortune favouring each side at different periods. This conflict was materially influenced, however, by many factors and complications. For one thing, imperial questions were inextricably related to domestic concerns and party politics. Significant differences of attitude could be discerned within the major political groupings, and at certain moments it did matter for the handling of colonial questions which parties and persons were in power in Britain. Furthermore, some historians had tended to ignore the fact that Victorian attitudes to empire were compounded of more elements than self-interest. While commercial considerations were always powerful, the existence of a missionary spirit and mere jingoism could not be discounted as important influences, especially amongst such groups as the radical imperialists or Colonial Reformers. Another complication was that both advocates and critics of empire supported their cases by appealing to the identical grounds of economic interest, national honour, and Christian principle. With such complications and volatile materials involved, British opinion on imperial issues was bound to be diverse and fluctuating; thus the use of labels and descriptions which implied uniformity and continuity was highly misleading.

Closer study of what contemporaries actually said and wrote has certainly shown that the casual use of conventional labels has tended to obscure the diversity and subtlety of public opinion and to encourage the perpetuation of misleading myths. A good example of this is the term, the 'Manchester school', which has traditionally been employed to describe an attitude that was favourable to free trade and hostile to colonies. William D. Grampp in his book, *The Manchester School of Economics* (Stanford, 1960), however, conclusively argued that the term included a variety of self-interested and humanitarian businessmen, pacifists, utilitarians, and middle-class radicals, whose opinions and objectives were by no means identical. Free traders could be found but no 'school' existed before the campaign to abolish the corn laws began in 1838, and after their repeal in 1846 the movement consisted of the followers of Cobden and Bright, who had some similarity of ideas but no specific purpose or common set of beliefs. Even between 1838 and 1846, when repeal provided a temporary unifying force, the Manchester radicals could not be legitimately described as a school because there was no relatively complete or consistent doctrine nor an authoritative statement of their views on particular issues.

Grampp therefore objected to the use of the term 'Manchester school' as synonymous either with the supporters of free trade after 1846 or with the followers of Cobden and Bright. Moreover, according to Grampp's own usage, the Manchester school had virtually nothing to do with colonies. Admittedly, the philosophic radicals included supporters of colonial reform, such as Molesworth, Roebuck, and Grote, but it also included Hume and Place who were critical of colonial possessions. At a later date, Cobden and other pacifists savagely attacked Palmerston for his aggressive and meddlesome foreign policies, and it was the activities of this group which gained for the Manchester school its reputation for being hostile to colonies and the empire. Nevertheless, Grampp maintained that this judgment represented an oversimplification of the views of the Manchester radicals, since this hostility was confined to Cobdenites and pacifists and was not representative of other elements of the school.

WAGNER, SEMMEL, AND WINCH: CLASSICAL ECONOMISTS, PHILOSOPHIC RADICALS, AND EMPIRE

Although Gallagher and Robinson had declared mid Victorian anti-imperialism to be a myth, historians had not yet satisfactorily decided whether the empire expanded with the support of public opinion or despite the criticisms and hostility of contemporaries. Much recent inquiry in this respect has been concerned with the views of the classical economists, the Benthamite radicals, and others who have traditionally appeared as critics or sceptics in the history of British imperialism, and who attacked the evils of the old colonial system in Canada and elsewhere in the light of the new science of political economy. It might of course be argued that economists and other theorists exercised an indecisive influence for or against imperial expansion, but historians have recently attempted to show that the majority of economists during those years, or at least after about 1830, were not in fact anti-imperialists, and that while they criticized the old colonial system, they were not universally hostile to empire as such.

An early challenge to the accepted view was put forward by Donald O. Wagner, in the first of two articles on "British Economists and the Empire", *Political Science Quarterly*, XLVI, 1931, 248-76. He argued that economists in the late eighteenth and early nineteenth centuries expressed divergent views concerning the value of colonies, even though they almost unanimously condemned the old colonial system. In the 1830's, however, an imperialist revival occurred. Its progenitors, who emphasized the value of emigration and colonization for the alleviation of Britain's domestic difficulties, were Malthus, Bentham, James Mill, Torrens, McCulloch, and Horton. Nevertheless, they differed widely over the value of overseas possessions, the wisdom of emancipating colonies, and the reforms needed to remedy the defects of the old colonial system. The arrival of Wakefield as the new prophet of colonies and colonization profoundly altered the attitudes of the classical economists. The initial reaction to Wakefield's ideas was mixed, with McCulloch and Horton hostile, John Stuart Mill, Nassau Senior, and Herman Merivale favourable, Bentham at first sceptical but later won over. But after 1831 the old school of colonial critics disappeared as most economists became advocates of colonies only if free trade and local autonomy were first established.

Wagner therefore implied that most economists became supporters of Wakefield's views on colonies and colonization after 1830 and that these views predominated between 1830 and 1860, though little evidence was produced to substantiate these contentions. Moreover, Wagner did not cite the opinions of any economists during these years except those of Wakefield himself; thus Wakefield's many critics were ignored. These are the basic defects in Wagner's potentially important thesis that the economists of the period were not anti-imperialists. In view of the date at which the article was written, however, the answer provided is less surprising than the fact that the question was posed at all.

The theme was later taken up by Bernard Semmel in an article, "The Philosophic Radicals and Colonialism", *Journal of Economic History*, XXI, 1961, 513-25. Semmel was concerned with the views of the Benthamite or philosophic radicals, and he maintained that, far from being ideological opponents of colonialism, as Schuyler and other writers had depicted them, they were advocates of positive programmes of empire. With their arguments grounded in economic theory, they demonstrated the necessity of empire to Britain's industrial economy. It was well known, Semmel argued, that the Benthamite colonial reformers were advocates of colonies and colonization, but they also emphasized the fact that the processes of the new industrial capitalism made it essential for Britain to possess undeveloped lands overseas which could receive surplus capital and population, and which would open up markets for the excess capacity of British factories. Moreover, it was argued that without a positive programme to extend the field of production in this way, Britain faced disastrous social revolution.

As early as the 1830's, Wakefield had fully grasped this situation and his diagnosis and remedies adumbrated certain ideas later associated with Marx. Wakefield's general theory of colonization became part of the programme of the leading philosophic radicals with the conversion of Bentham and the more influential of his followers, including James and John Stuart Mill, Molesworth, Buller, and Grote. With fears of political democracy and inharmonious industrialism, the philosophic radicals advocated an imperial programme in the thirties and forties to relieve mounting social pressures in Britain. Moreover, Semmel believed that their views on the value of colonies were influential in mid Victorian England in urging a rather lethargic public and government to undertake more positive imperial activities, more influential, in fact, than the negative concept of empire entertained by Cobden and the Manchester radicals. The ideas of the Cobdenites conformed more nearly to the traditional views of a mid Victorian anti-colonialism, but, Semmel argued, despite the misleading adoption of Cobdenite cant by leading British statesmen, their opinions did not generally prevail.

The major weakness of this thesis is the assumption that the terms 'Benthamite radical', 'philosophic radical', 'colonial reformer', and 'Wakefieldian' are synonymous and can be used interchangeably. Not all the Benthamites can legitimately be described as colonial reformers, and not everyone would agree that Wakefield was a radical. Moveover, the thesis is not as original as Semmel claimed, since earlier writers had not described the colonial reformers as hostile to empire. Nor had Wakefield's scheme of colonization as a positive imperial programme designed to relieve British social and economic difficulties been ignored by earlier writers even though Schuyler had given insufficient weight to this consideration. Semmel's article therefore reinforces the point that, while it is essential to ascertain what contemporaries actually said and wrote, the perpetuation of vague labels to categorize opinion can be more misleading than instructive.

The attitude of the classical economists to colonies was examined along similar lines by Donald N. Winch, particularly in his "Classical Economics and the Case for Colonization", *Economica*, XXX, 1963, 387-99, and *Classical Political Economy and Colonies* (London, 1965). Winch argued that in the years between 1776 and the 1860's, the classical school of political economy subjected every facet of colonial policy to the logic of economic analysis and to the more general criteria associated with the principle of utility. Until 1830, the economists and their Benthamite colleagues remained critics of the concept of empire implied in the old colonial system because mercantilist principles offended liberal values. But after 1830 with the advent of

Wakefield's plan of colonization and the growth of the colonial reform movement, the attitude of the classical economists to colonies gradually changed from hostility, or at best scepticism, to enthusiasm.

During the course of this debate, colonial questions often became a battleground for differences of opinion on wider matters of economic analysis and policy. Winch examined how the economic problems raised by colonies and colonization went to the root of classical inquiry, with discussion of free trade, capital accumulation, population pressure, economic growth, and the role of the state. After 1830, economists tried to show that colonization would resolve Britain's domestic difficulties without the undesirable side-effects feared by previous writers on emigration, and that colonies so established would be free from the economic and political disadvantages criticized by earlier members of the classical school. The case for extending or disbanding the empire did not therefore, turn exclusively on economic arguments, and writers made both political and economic judgments in their assessment of the value of colonies to Britain. Winch stressed that the movement for colonial reform was a product of philosophic radicalism and an attempt to transplant Benthamite political ideas in a new setting. Colonization was not regarded simply as an economic remedy for British and colonial difficulties, but as a means of creating a new type of society and demonstrating that an empire could be built as the fulfilment of liberal values, and not as an aberration from them. Although the views of economists were not set in the wider context of British opinion, nor compared and contrasted with contemporary attitudes to empire, Winch claimed that the leading economists of the period whose support Wakefield was able to obtain, contributed greatly to the rise of liberal imperialism.

JOHN S. GALBRAITH:
"MYTHS OF THE 'LITTLE ENGLAND' ERA" (1961)

Criticisms of the traditional interpretation of British attitudes to empire in the second quarter of the nineteenth century were effectively brought together in the seminal article by John S. Galbraith, "Myths of the 'Little England' Era", **American Historical Review**, LXVII, 1961, 34-48. The article represented a protest against the uncritical repetition of accepted explanations and the widespread use of labels in imperial history which did nothing to clarify the groups or opinions being described. So many writers from Seeley's day to the present had based their accounts on the work of a previous 'authority' whose study was also derivative. Time and repetition had sanctified many generalizations which, on closer inquiry, proved to be undocumented, exaggerated, or untrue. This tendency was particularly evident in interpretations of the second and third quarters of the nineteenth century, conventionally called the 'Little England' era.

Between 1815 and 1870, according to the traditional view, mercantilism gradually gave way to free trade. As it did so, merchants and industrialists came to regard with increasing repugnance an empire sustained before 1849 by a system of preferential customs duties, and, both before and after the repeal of the Navigation Laws, protected by troops at the expense of the British taxpayer. Britain's industrial supremacy led to the withdrawal of imperial subsidies for colonial government and defence, because the empire no longer provided significant countervailing commercial advantages. If the logical outcome of colonial self-support proved to be secession, many Englishmen would have welcomed this result. Those who held these views had usually been described as 'Little Englanders' or 'Separationists', and for thirty years after 1840 this attitude, though with variations, was thought to have prevailed in Britain, not only amongst theorists and writers, but also amongst leading politicians and imperial administrators.

Like most distortions, Galbraith admitted that this description of British opinion and policy contained a grain of truth. Some writers did denounce the empire as an expensive anachronism, and some statesmen in moments of exasperation often produced by an unproductive but expensive colonial war, described colonies as burdens. But he maintained that no responsible ministers during the 'Little England' era endorsed the view that the separation of the colonies from Britain would be desirable. It was significant that the label of 'Little Englander' was applied to politicians by opponents, not to themselves or their friends. Moreover, the attempt by historians to portray a statesman's views from a study of his public speeches or private letters could be hazardous, since the most contradictory conclusions could be reached by the partial selection of material from speeches and writings. Galbraith cited as examples the conventional judgments on Cobden and Gladstone. Cobden was usually regarded as the personification of 'Little Englandism', but he in fact repudiated such doctrines, though his words, when taken out of context, sometimes suggested that he wanted Britain to be rid of colonies. Like the Manchester school of which he was often a spokesman, Cobden did not express a consistent point of view with regard to imperial policy. His advocacy of free trade and international peace affected his attitude to empire, but on imperial questions generally Galbraith considered him relatively uninformed. Since his views varied according to the occasion and particular circumstances, he might sound like an enlightened imperialist or suspiciously like a separatist. Similarly, historians had often labelled Gladstone a 'Little Englander', but during his long career he gained a more sympathetic and statesmanlike view of imperial relations than most of his contemporaries. By 1850, he had become convinced that paternalistic control and constant interference from London were disadvantageous to Britain and degrading to the colonists. The proper relationship between Britain and the colonies should be based on mutual interests, common ideals, and familial sentiments.

When the evidence for charges of separatism against politicians was examined, Galbraith noted that these accusations usually related to criticisms of colonial expenditure or the continued possession of British North America. Since Canadian problems preoccupied the attention of ministries and parliament in the period from 1830 to 1860 more than the affairs of any other part of the empire except India, it was not surprising that historians had interpreted critical comments on these issues as a reflection of a general scepticism about the empire at large. Many writers and politicians suggested that British North America was a liability, especially at times when Anglo-American relations were strained, and the exposure of Canada to American attack created embarrassment for Britain so long as there was a responsibility for its defence. Galbraith pointed out, however, that no minister ever expressed these sentiments, even in private correspondence with trusted friends. On the contrary, every ministry, of whatever shade of political opinion, sought to preserve the connection and prevent Canada from falling into the hands of the United States, which would have involved an aggrandisement of American power and the extension of American trade barriers against British manufactured goods. Although various British politicians offered different solutions to Canada's problems, they were unanimous in agreeing that Canada belonged within the British rather than the American orbit.

In common with Gallagher and Robinson, Galbraith believed that the myth of the 'Little England' era stemmed largely from historians' preoccupation with empire in a strictly political sense and their failure to appreciate the importance of the 'informal empire' of trade and investment. The early Victorians were apathetic or hostile to the expansion of formal empire because political control meant an expensive responsibility for administration and defence. Englishmen decidedly preferred to promote trade and investment without such expense. Between 1815 and 1870, international conditions favoured a more relaxed, informal policy than was possible in the later years of the century. Britain enjoyed an unparalleled freedom of access to the markets of the world, an absence of commercial competitors, and no shortage of eager buyers of British manufactured goods and capital equipment. In these circumstances, with a large part of the world drawn into the British sphere of commercial influence, there was no need for the assertion of political sovereignty over new dependencies and the expensive appurtenances of imperial administration.

If the term 'Little Englander' was misleading as a description of a significant British attitude to empire, so also was the label 'Colonial Reformer'. Superficially, the colonial reformers appeared a more distinct and coherent group because their spokesmen vigorously expounded the evils of paternalism and the benefits of self-government. But Galbraith considered it characteristic that the reformers should have sought to emphasize the virtues of their arguments by exaggerating the defects and shortsightedness of their opponents, as in Buller's caricature of Stephen and Wakefield's bitter attacks on Wilmot Horton and Earl Grey. By the creation of their own distorted image of their opponents, the colonial reformers contributed materially to the myth of the 'Little Englander' as the antithesis of their own enlightened outlook. Galbraith argued, however, that the ideas they advocated were very similar to the views of those they vehemently denounced. The reformers maintained that the grant of self-government would bind the colonies to Britain by bonds of interest and affection and that self-administering colonies must be able to maintain themselves and no longer be a burden on the imperial treasury. With some differences in emphasis, this view would have been endorsed by most British politicians of the day.

The antithesis of 'Colonial Reformer' and 'Little Englander', therefore, bore no relation to reality. Molesworth, for example, had conventionally been described as a reformer, but the ideas expressed in his writings and speeches were often indistinguishable from those attributed to the separatists. At a time when the world was eager to trade and Britain did not need to buy customers for its products, he became increasingly critical of colonial expenditure for which there seemed no economic return. In striking contrast to Canada, which involved only embarrassment and expense, he emphasized that the independent United States were more profitable to Britain than all its colonies combined. Although the logic of these arguments appeared to imply that secession was desirable, Molesworth refused to draw this conclusion. He contended that if colonies were self-governing and self-supporting, with Britain simply protecting the oceanic trade routes, the bonds of empire would in fact be strengthened. Molesworth therefore sought, not the end of empire, but the end of expensive paternalism.

The spectrum of opinion on colonies, Galbraith concluded, was much narrower than the language of partisan politics seemed to suggest. There was in fact very little difference in the views of such politicians as Gladstone, Grey, Molesworth, and Russell. For this reason, the labels 'Little Englander', 'Colonial Reformer', and 'Liberal Imperialist' obscured rather than facilitated an understanding of British attitudes and policy. Such terms suggested a clash of opposites and produced a false impression of symmetry which on examination did not correspond to the facts. It would be equally wrong, to stress the similarity rather than the diversity of opinion, Galbraith argued, since British attitudes to empire and imperial policy in the nineteenth century were characterized by inconsistencies and contradictions which seemed to defy coherent analysis.

CONCLUSION

Even if they have not been exclusively or directly related to British North America, recent studies have effectively challenged the traditional view of British attitudes to empire in the early and mid nineteenth century. But if long accepted explanations are no longer tenable, a new synthesis has yet to emerge. This may prove to be a slow and difficult process because viable generalizations about British opinion and colonies will have to recognize all manners of discrepancies and inconsistencies which earlier historians deliberately or unconsciously ignored. Nevertheless, certain prerequisites for future studies can be stated and some lines of fruitful inquiry can be suggested.

Both the defects and the persistence of the traditional explanations of Bodelsen and Schuyler can largely be traced to the plausibility of the propaganda assiduously broadcast by Wakefield and his associates, and to the wholesale, uncritical acceptance by later writers of Wakefield's partisan views and his oversimplified picture of contemporary opinions and practices as an accurate account of the period. Wakefield's spell must be broken. This point, which formed the starting point of H. T. Manning's article, "Who Ran the British Empire—1830-1850?", *Journal of British Studies*, V, 1965, 88-121, has recently been elaborated by A. G. L. Shaw in "British Attitudes to the Colonies, ca. 1820-1850", *Journal of British Studies*, IX, 1969, 71-95. Although the scope of the latter article is more restricted than its broad title misleadingly suggests, Shaw examined and dismissed the assertions of the Wakefieldians that parliament was uninterested in colonial problems, and that because secretaries of state were incompetent or held office for brief periods, the empire was run by permanent officials at the Colonial Office. The article covered a limited range of English opinion and dealt only with the familiar issues of colonial land, emigration, and government, but it demonstrated that future explanations must be based on the exhaustive canvass and critical evaluation of all available sources, and must reflect what contemporaries actually said and not the views attributed to them by later writers. Comments must accordingly be interpreted within the context of the circumstances in which they were made, and the changes and contradictions in the opinions of individuals over a period of time must be acknowledged.

Whether or not conventional labels and categories are entirely discarded, the sharp contrast traditionally drawn between critics and supporters of empire, between 'imperialists' and 'anti-imperialists', must be abandoned. Attitudes differed according to the issue under consideration—whether it related to the machinery of imperial administration at home or overseas, commercial relations, colonial defence, or some other aspect of imperial affairs. Colonial Reformers favoured self-government but criticized imperial expenditure on colonial defence; Benthamites and classical economists condemned the old colonial system but were not averse to all aspects of empire. In the article, "Parliamentary Radicals and the Reduction of Imperial Expenditure in British North America, 1827-1834", *Historical Journal*, XI, 1968, 446-61, this author has argued that Joseph Hume and the radicals in the House of Commons during the late twenties and early thirties were not hostile to colonies as such, as has usually been asserted, and that their campaign for economy and the devolution of imperial authority represented as constructive a programme for the empire as that propounded by the

Colonial Reformers. In order to create a new synthesis, it must be recognized that British opinion was characterized by similarities, diversities, and inconsistencies, and cannot therefore be reduced to tidy order. A more fruitful approach might thus be to take issues and themes, rather than chronological periods and amorphous groups of individuals, as the future framework for examining attitudes to empire. More would be learned about British opinion by analysing different views on such topics as the Canadian timber duties, colonial church establishments, the dispute over the Maine border, or the rebellions of 1837, than by straining the evidence to establish the prevailing mood of an age or the consistent and enduring attitudes of a particular, though indistinct, group.

The analysis of British opinion must also in future be more closely related to imperial policy and developments overseas. It is meaningless to study opinion in isolation, divorced from the actual course of events, and to describe the period under consideration as an age of anti-imperialism when in fact colonial trade, overseas investment, and territorial possessions expanded so significantly. What is needed is an assessment of how far and in what ways government policies were variously affected by such factors as contemporary opinion, the demands of British commercial interests, and the inexorable pressure of circumstances on the colonial frontiers of trade and settlement. Certainly historians have mistakenly seen policy as something formulated in London and have thus neglected the compelling force of local exigencies and the activities of the man on the spot. If these various factors are taken into consideration, the course of imperial activity might well show a continuing, if intermittent, struggle between the hopes of limiting or reducing commitments and the realities of increasing involvement or territorial expansion, between desirable economy and enforced expenditure. In the course of this struggle, the existence of hostile or favourable opinion in parliament, in the press, or amongst the public at large might not on many occasions have exerted a decisive influence over the policy of the government, and if effective at other times, might either have restrained or precipitated action. It should always be remembered that British ministers and officials dealt pragmatically with colonial problems as they arose, and while official decisions reflected private attitudes as well as expediency, these decisions were seldom affected by a public opinion that generally remained too indifferent or ill-informed to be influential. In his book, *British Colonial*

Administration in the Mid-Nineteenth Century: The Policy-Making Process (New Haven, 1970), J. W. Cell has argued that policy formation was a complex process that represented a fluctuating set of responses by officials to the continuous interaction among people, ideas, the speeches of Victorian politicians on colonial affairs, but also the tendency of individuals to label their opponents, and not themselves, as separatists and Little Englanders. Since denunciation of colonial expenditure and the burdens of empire formed standard slogans of the forces, and institutions. In addition to some novel comments on the genesis, working, and implications of responsible government in Canada and other colonies of European settlement, Cell's study underlines the need for more case studies of particular issues and of developments in various parts of the empire, in order to assess the various determinants of policy making and the relative influence of ideas and public opinion.

Furthermore, the different colonial possessions have to be treated as individual cases. The problems and situation of British North America were not identical to those of any other territory due to the presence there of British settlers, growing political independence, a continuing imperial military commitment, and proximity to the United States. A series of local and regional studies is needed before it is possible to ascertain how far British attitudes and policy to Canada reflected attitudes and policies to the empire at large, and how far they were individual to British North America. Earlier writers considered the frequent criticism of British possessions in North America as conclusive evidence of a prevailing indifference or hostility to the colonial empire as such; but the situation in Canada was unique rather than typical of British possessions in general, because the process of devolution and imperial withdrawal demanded by many Englishmen, as well as by Canadians, could be accomplished in Canada with greater safety than in any other part of the contemporary empire. Neither critical nor favourable views of the British commitment in the settlement colonies of North America can therefore be taken as an accurate reflection of English attitudes to imperial activities in South Africa, Australasia, India, or the vast informal commercial empire so long ignored by writers on imperial history.

In the assessment of public opinion, allowance must also be made for the rhetoric used by British politicians and polemic writers. Views expressed during partisan political speeches and during outbursts of irritation should not be interpreted too literally, since rhetorical stances did not necessarily reflect the true personal beliefs of individuals or their more stable, responsible modes of political behaviour. This common phenomenon has often been forgotten by imperial historians, but to a large extent it explains not only the disparity and inconsistencies in day, and were recognized as such, this may account in part for the palpable lack of influence exerted by economisers and pessimists over imperial policy and practice. It also suggests why radicals remained the most outspoken critics of colonial burdens. Throughout the period under consideration, it is obvious that ministers and leading politicians, Whig and Tory, who held office or aspired to it, evinced more favourable and responsible attitudes to empire than did radicals, outsiders, and those permanently excluded from political office, who could afford to be outspoken and indulge in rhetoric without the likelihood of being called upon to put their views into effect. At the same time, as J. S. Galbraith has observed in the article discussed earlier, the range of opinion on colonies was much narrower than the language of partisan politics might suggest to the casual observer. At the extremes of the political spectrum the radicals remained the most bitter critics of empire and Tory imperialists its most fervent advocates, though the views of the latter have not been accorded the importance they deserve because historians have not read the Tory press of the day. But in the wide, common ground at the centre of British politics, responsibility for governing the empire, or the possibility of exercising it, had a sobering effect and made politicians, if not their partisan supporters, more sympathetic to colonial possessions, more fearful of the United States, and more conscious of the need to maintain British power and interests in North America and other crucial areas.

The essential debate amongst those in the mainstream of English politics therefore concerned, not the wisdom or desirability of these imperial objectives, but the most appropriate means of achieving them. While criticism of the methods adopted for the pursuit of agreed objectives might on occasion lead to a revision or abandonment of the government's current tactics, ministers could usually count on wide support in parliament and from the press for the underlying principles of imperial policy. This made it easier for successive ministries to ignore critical voices which they felt were irresponsible or unrepresentative. Most Englishmen regarded British interests as paramount in the sphere of colonial policy and imperial relations. In the commercial reforms of the period, only the interests of the mother country were effectively consulted, though many supporters of free trade believed that the abolition of protection would promote the welfare of the colonists. In political matters, similarly, colonial demands for self-government could be conceded in North America because informal control appeared to be the most efficacious means of achieving essential commercial and strategic objectives by the 1840's. Canada, in fact, represented a classic example of the transition from formal to informal empire, where British administrative and financial commitments could be safely reduced to a minimum, despite a continuing fear of American ambitions. This transition was accompanied by frequent complaints concerning the burdens of the North American empire, by much favourable comment on the value of those provinces, and by considerable uncertainty about the future course of Britain's relations with them. Yet British attitudes must be seen in perspective: Canada remained part of the empire because the colonists wished to preserve the connection. In this and in other ways, the practical realities of conditions in the colonies contributed as much to the process of devolution as did public opinion in England, however sympathic or critical it may have been towards Britain's empire in North America.